GARDENERS' WORLD

BOOK OF

HOUSE
PLANTS

ANNE SWITHINBANK

BBC BOOKS

CREDITS

I would like to thank the following, who very kindly lent plants and containers for photographic purposes:

The Bulb Information Desk,
Highland Hall,
Renwick,
Penrith,
Cumbria CA10 1JL

Chessington Nurseries Ltd,
Leatherhead Road,
Chessington,
Surrey
(0372 720260)
(retail)

Keith Butters Ltd,
Kellet Gate,
Spalding,
Lincolnshire PE12 6EH
(0775 768831)
(wholesale)

Linnells Plants Ltd,
Linnells Nurseries,
Hurst Lane,
Egham,
Surrey TW20 8QJ
(0784 437677)
(wholesale)

Natural Way Ltd,
Guildford Road,
Cranleigh,
Surrey GU6 8LT
(0483 272560)
(wholesale)

RHS Enterprises Ltd,
RHS Gardens,
Wisley,
Woking,
Surrey GU23 6QB
(0483 211113)
(retail)

Stuart Lowe Ltd,
Park View Nursery,
Theobalds Park Road,
Crews Hill,
Enfield,
Middlesex EN2 9BQ
(081 363 0104)
(wholesale)

PLANT POT CONTAINERS
WERE SUPPLIED BY

Clandon Park Garden Centre,
Clandon Park,
West Clandon,
Surrey
(0483 222925)
(retail)

Stewart Products,
Purley Way,
Croydon CR9 4HS
(081 686 2231)
(wholesale)

Published by BBC Books,
a division of BBC Enterprises Limited,
Woodlands, 80 Wood Lane, London W12 0TT
First published 1991
© Anne Swithinbank 1991
Line illustrations © Kate Simunek 1991
All photographs © Jon Bouchier 1991 except
p. 9 (left) Oxford Scientific Films (Stan Osolinski);
p. 9 (right) Anne Swithinbank; p. 122 (left)
A-Z Botanical Collection; p. 122 (right) and pp. 121,
123, 124 Holt Studios (Nigel Cattlin).
ISBN 0 563 20780 9
Set in Kennerley by Ace Filmsetting Ltd, Frome
Printed and bound in England by Clays Ltd, St Ives Plc
Colour separations by Technik Ltd, Berkhamsted
Cover printed by Clays Ltd, St Ives Plc

CONTENTS

Overleaf: Temporary houseplants like (from top left clockwise) *Primula malacoides*, *Cineraria*, *Calceolaria* and *Campanula* are short-lived and best viewed as a long-lasting bunch of flowers.

1

A BEGINNER'S GUIDE

BUYING HOUSE PLANTS

Whether you are choosing plants from a garden centre or florist's, for yourself or as a gift, a little extra thought could save problems later. I always find it helps to divide house plants up into two categories. There are what I think of as permanent house plants which, well cared for, should last for years in the home. These are often foliage plants like *Dieffenbachia* (dumb cane), *Monstera* (Swiss cheese plant) and *Ficus benjamina* (weeping fig), although some, like *Anthurium* (flamingo flower), *Clivia* (kaffir lily) and *Beloperone* (shrimp plant) have flowers as well. You will have time to learn skills like pruning and taking cuttings, to make your plants last even longer. Temporary house plants are either annuals or short-lived plants, which are thrown away when they have flowered, like *Cineraria*, *Calceolaria* and *Campanula*. They can also be those plants which cannot live in the house all year round or need a dormant period. Some knowledge and skill will be involved in keeping them going from year to year by placing them in the garden during

summer or allowing them to die down for a rest period. These include *Cyclamen*, azalea, *Cymbidium*, *Achimenes* (hot water plant) and *Hippeastrum* (amaryllis).

As you walk around the tempting displays of plants, try and work out whether you want to take home a colourful potful which will give you a few weeks of colour, rather like a long-lasting bunch of flowers, or a permanent house plant which, well cared for, will become a long-term resident.

For a good-quality temporary house plant bought for its flowering potential, choose one which is just beginning to open its flowers and has lots of buds in reserve. The rest of the plant should be sturdy, healthy and should not rock around in its pot. For a good permanent house plant you should look, above all, for sturdy, compact and healthy growth. If you are buying a plant that flowers as well as producing attractive leaves, try not to be led astray by numbers of flowers. Look beyond them to the quality of the leaves and stems, particularly an abundance of healthy shoots on a well-balanced plant. Long after the flowers have faded you will be left with the quality of plant you have chosen.

Many of us buy house plants during winter to brighten up our homes. Do not forget that these plants are not hardy. Never carry a plant outside into freezing temperatures or cold winds unless it has been well wrapped. Good garden centres will have all the right wrappings at their disposal so make sure that they use them. Never leave plants in cars during freezing conditions as cars are not warm enough to keep out frost. This might sound obvious but a friend of mine once absent-mindedly left a beautiful foliage plant intended as a gift in her car overnight and was then most surprised when it died soon after. On hot, sunny days cars are much too warm and, if left too long inside, house plants will become baked.

House plants make very welcome gifts and the choice is wide. Naturally, one should try and choose what the recipient might like rather than what one would choose for oneself. We made a *Gardeners' World* programme from a garden centre where we helped schoolchildren choose plants for Mothers' Day. This was most enjoyable and hilarious. Many of the boys tried to outdo each other in choosing the ugliest, spikiest cactus. A cactus-lover myself, I would have been the last person to put them off but I did try to make them think whether that would have been their mother's first choice. Children do like

curious plants like cacti, *Lithops* (pebble plants), carnivorous plants and air plants. Elderly people tend to live in rather warm rooms, so unless they have a porch, avoid plants like *Cyclamen* and azaleas which collapse in high temperatures. African violets, *Streptocarpus* (Cape primrose) and poinsettias would be more suitable. Students, on the other hand, often live in cold rooms because they cannot afford the heating (I really found out what minimum temperatures were when I was training at the Royal Botanic Gardens, Kew). They tend to prefer large, tough foliage plants like *Yucca*, *Scindapsus* (devil's ivy), palms and *Aspidistra*.

POSITIONING THE PLANTS

The first major decision you have to make about your new purchase is where it is going to live in the house. I am afraid that unless you have money to waste and are hardhearted, aesthetics must come second. Your new *Nephrolepis* (Boston fern) may well look magnificent draped over the small table in the corner but if it happens to be next door to a radiator the fern will soon turn brown and dry. A *Citrus* in a decorative pot might well be just right for the dining room but will it receive the light it needs for strong, healthy growth? Before finding the right spot, take a good look at the plant and read its label. Never come away from the shop or garden centre without a name to your plant, otherwise you will not be able to find out any information about it. The A to Z section of this book covers most of the house plants you are likely to buy. If your geography is good, sometimes just knowing where the plant comes from in the wild will help to identify its particular needs. Many foliage plants come from tropical rain forests where they are used to growing in the shade of the tree canopy. Some grow on the forest floor, some climb high up into the trees, and others are epiphytic, meaning that they find a niche in the branches of the trees or in a fissure of bark where they can take a roothold and grow. These epiphytes do not usually have a well-developed root system and can absorb what they need from the atmosphere around them and drips from the leaves above. They are certainly not parasites and take no nourishment from the tree they cling to. While these forest plants make good house plants as they can grow in filtered light, they usually need a warm, stable temperature and humidity.

Some house plants are natives of parts of the world like the Mediterranean or South Africa. Soils in these regions tend to be well drained and rather poor while light is intense. These plants will need a sunny windowsill, will hate being over-watered and will prefer a dry atmosphere to a humid one.

If you know what sort of conditions your plants experience in the wild, like these desert cacti, it will help you understand how to care for them.

In the wild, *Philodendron* and *Monstera* will climb up tall trees, sending out aerial roots. No wonder they can sometimes threaten to take over your living-room.

CARE

WATERING

Having decided where your plant will be best placed in the house so that it is receiving the right light and temperature, the next hurdle lies in learning when and how much to water. As a general guide, feel the surface of the compost. When you can no longer squeeze moisture between your fingers and the compost begins to feel dry, then the plant is ready to be watered. There are exceptions to this rule. Some plants, notably ferns and azaleas, should be kept continuously moist, though never standing in water. Cacti and succulents, *Pelargoniums* and *Sansevieria* should be left until their compost is quite dry on the surface between waterings. When you decide to water, do so thoroughly. I water most of my plants from the top until water has penetrated right down through the pot, reaching all the roots. In time you will learn when to stop so that you do not leave too much of a puddle in the saucer, because this must be emptied out soon afterwards. The worst thing you can do is water little and often with an eggcupful of water each time. This will only moisten the surface, while roots towards the bottom die off. Plants that I think should be watered from the bottom, by filling the saucer, include African violets, *Streptocarpus* (Cape primrose) and *Cyclamen*. The saucer must be emptied when the plant has taken up as much water as it needs (usually after an hour). Whenever possible, use water that is at room temperature. Do not overwater as this effectively drowns the roots by preventing air circulation in the compost. The drowned roots die off, the plant cannot absorb water through them and collapses.

FEEDING

Most house plants need regular liquid feeds to keep them healthy. Permanent house plants may spend many years in the same pot, exhausting the supply of fertiliser in the compost. A general rule is to feed most house plants every two weeks while in healthy, active growth, usually between March and October. For plants that produce some winter growth, a monthly feed is usually adequate. There are many different feeds to choose from. Either use a good, general fertiliser or a specific one for your type of plant. There are feeds for foliage house plants, flowering house plants, cacti, orchids and African violets. For the absent-minded, slow-release fertilisers are the solution. These come as sticks, tablets or granules and, once applied, usually last at least six weeks before they need renewing. To give a plant a quick pick-me-up, a foliar feed is the answer, best applied by misting the feed, diluted into water, over and under the foliage. A newly potted plant will not require feeding for about six weeks as it will find all it needs in its new compost and must build up a new, active root system. Never feed a plant that is bone dry.

HUMIDITY

Dry air during winter is a real problem for some house plants. Stress is usually indicated by dry tips to the leaves and falling flower buds. Humidity can be increased by grouping plants together as they all give off moisture from their leaves and compost. Alternatively, stand the plants on wide saucers containing pebbles. Keep the pebbles moist by maintaining a water level just below the base of the pot. The plant must not stand in water but benefit from the evaporation around it. Regular misting with a fine spray will increase humidity.

REPOTTING

Many house-plant growers are confused about when they should repot. If you want your house plant to grow fast, then when you feel that the roots have filled the present pot (you can usually see them coming out of the bottom and can tap the rootball out to see), pot on into two sizes larger, for example, a 4-inch (10-cm) to a 6-inch (15-cm) pot. Pot on in spring or early summer so that the plants can develop a strong root system before the low-light and harsher conditions of winter. Most permanent house plants can spend four or five years in the same pot without suffering, provided they have the light, water and feed that they need. Usually a plant will let you know

A *Maranta* enjoying the humidity given off by a wide saucer of moist pebbles.

Right: This *Radermachera* is obviously ready for potting on into a larger pot.

when it is pot-bound, by a stunted appearance and yellowing leaves. For most plants a multi-purpose or house-plant, peat-based compost is ideal. For plants that are succulent or like a hot, dry atmosphere, a soil-based compost is often more suitable. I like to add extra peat and grit (or sharp sand) to a John Innes No. 2 compost for these plants. For special groups like cacti, orchids and *Saintpaulias* (African violets) it is possible to buy specific composts. Never attempt to grow orchids in ordinary compost. Most need a special compost composed mainly of orchid-grade bark.

The potting process is simple. Place a small amount of new compost into a clean pot so that when you stand the old rootball on top, the surface of the old compost will be at the correct height to allow for watering. If the old rootball is very congested, gently tease a few roots away from the base and sides to give them a start. Gradually fill new compost around the old rootball, making sure that it is in the centre of the pot and the plant is upright. Firm gently. Give the old rootball surface the merest covering of compost, then tap the pot down on a hard surface to settle everything. Water in thoroughly.

CLEANING

Inevitably, house plants will collect dust which must be cleaned off regularly. Plants need to absorb light over their leaf surfaces in order to carry out photosynthesis, the process by which they release energy, en-

Potting on a Schlumbergera.

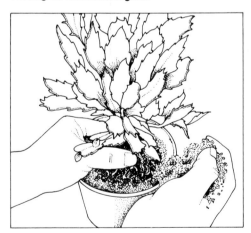

Put some new compost into the base of the pot, so that the plant will be at the correct height, and fill in around the old root ball with compost.

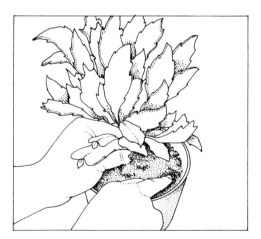

Hold the plant upright and at the right height with one hand while gently pressing in the new compost with the fingers of the other.

abling them to grow. I use a soft cloth or brush to remove dust gently before wiping with a moist cloth or cotton wool if this is necessary. New leaves are usually fragile and should be left until they are older before being cleaned. Some plants, particularly those with thick, shiny leaves, look smart if sprayed or wiped with one of the many house plant cleaning or shining products. Personally, I prefer plants to look natural, finding it incongruous when a naturally matt plant appears shiny. Do take care not to treat young or hairy leaves as these are easily damaged.

PROPAGATION

Beginner house plant growers may find that the challenge of keeping their plants alive and healthy is enough to start with. Before long curiosity will win and some knowledge of propagation will be needed to rejuvenate plants and grow spares to swap with friends. The best time to undertake any of the fol-lowing methods is late spring or early sum-mer when natural light and temperatures are on your side.

SEED AND SPORE SOWING

Seed sowing can be a technical process but this general method involves the minimum of equipment. For most seed, or pips, a 3½-inch (9-cm) pot is the ideal size. Fill with seed compost, press down lightly with a smooth, round surface and water using a can

fitted with a rose or by standing the pot in a pan of water for about an hour. Having achieved a smooth, moist surface, push large seed into this so that it is covered by its own size with compost. Small seed should be scattered thinly on the surface and either covered with the merest scattering of

Exotic fruits like citrus, mango, passion fruit and lychees are fun to grow from seed.

Most yield pips or stones which are easy to sow.

Space citrus pips out on the surface of some seed compost, then push in until they are covered by a depth of soil equal to their own size.

compost or not at all. Press lightly to bring the seed in contact with the compost, then label and stand the pot in a polythene bag. Loosely knot the bag and place it in good but not direct light. Germination times will vary between three to four days and over a year. Should there be any signs of drying out, stand in water until sufficient has been soaked up. Some seed might need higher temperatures than an ordinary room or require darkness to germinate. As soon as seedlings appear, remove the polythene and stand the pot on a light windowsill but not where the sun might scorch delicate leaves. When the seedlings have begun to grow their second set of leaves they can be pricked out individually into small pots. Remember to handle them only by their leaves to avoid damaging the stem.

Fern spores can be sown on to peat or peat-based seed compost prepared in the same way. Spores are dust-like and must be carefully scattered over the surface of the moist peat. Stand the pot in a saucer kept topped up with water and slip a polythene bag over the top. Place somewhere out of direct light and leave until a strange growth resembling liverworts covers the surface. This might take six months or longer but is the first stage in the fern's development. Soon, recognisable fronds will form and small patches can be transferred to individual pots. Later still, when the ferns can be distinguished from each other, they can be separated again.

SHOOT-TIP CUTTINGS

Most house plants can be propagated by removing shoot tips and encouraging them to root. Unless the plant is particularly large, these should be only 3 to 4 inches (7.5 to 10 cm) long. Select the healthiest material, remove from the plant and trim the cutting with a sharp knife just under a node (leaf joint). Remove the bottom leaves, dip into hormone rooting powder and insert into a small pot of cutting compost (equal amounts of peat and sharp sand or vermiculite). Fill the pot with several cuttings, then place in a polythene bag, knot loosely and stand out of direct light. As soon as roots have formed and the cuttings seem to be growing, take them from the bag, leave for a few days to acclimatise, then pot up separately. Some plants like cacti,

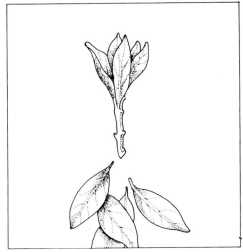

Shoot-tip cuttings of *Columnea.*
Select a healthy shoot tip and remove it from the parent plant.

Trim the cutting under a node (or leaf joint) and remove the bottom leaves.

Insert several cuttings into a small pot of cutting compost.

Water the cuttings in, then place inside a loosely knotted polythene bag, stand in good but not direct light.

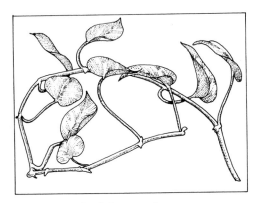

Different kinds of shoot cuttings.
This long stem of *Scindapsus* has no obvious shoot tip.

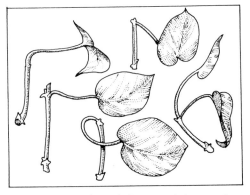

Many cuttings can be made by cutting below a node (leaf joint) at the base and above one at the top. Bottom leaves are removed.

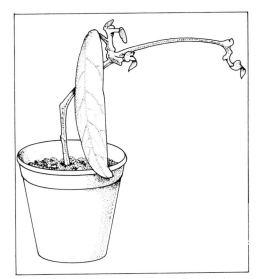

Hoyas can be awkward to take cuttings from, as they have long, wayward shoots not always with obvious growing tips. Cut below a node (leaf joint) at the base and a short length of stem will root and produce new shoots.

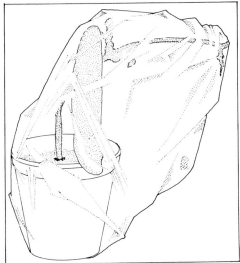

The *Hoya* cutting will appreciate the extra warmth and humidity provided by standing the pot inside a polythene bag.

succulents and pelargoniums must not be covered with polythene òr they will rot. Some cuttings (*Tradescantia*, *Begonia*, *Maranta*, *Fittonia* and many others) can be rooted in water. Fill an old glass almost to the top with water, place aluminium foil over the top and make small holes through which to poke the stems of the cuttings. The leaves will sit on top while the base of the stem, from which roots will form, is under water.

LEAF CUTTINGS

Several plants can be propagated by their leaves. African violets are well known for this. Select a healthy leaf approaching full development from about the middle of the plant. Cut away from the parent plant with stalk attached and trim to 1 inch (2.5 cm) for insertion into compost but longer to root in water. Use a sharp knife or razor blade to make a diagonal cut which will give a greater surface from which roots can form. Leaves rooted in water are best potted before plantlets form. Rooting in cutting compost is equally successful. Insert the leaf stems up to the leaf blade. Water in, sit inside a loosely knotted polythene bag and keep out of direct sunlight. Once plantlets have formed, wait until they are quite large before separating them into individual plants of single crowns. Some peperomias, too, will root from leaf cuttings, notably *P. caperata* and *P. argyreia*. I find that they are best rooted in cutting compost.

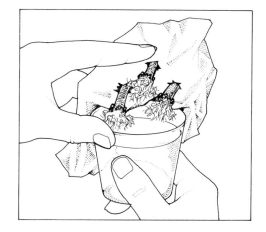

Top: *Saintpaulia* leaves will root well in water.

Many cuttings will root in water. Place aluminium foil over an old glass filled with water. Insert cuttings through holes in the foil so that the stems rest in the water and leaves are supported by the foil.

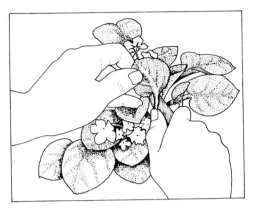

Leaf cuttings of *Saintpaulia*.
Select a healthy leaf from the middle of the plant.

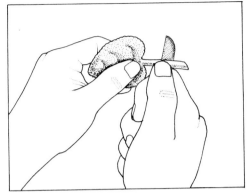

Trim the leaf stalk to about 1 inch (2.5 cm) long, making a diagonal cut.

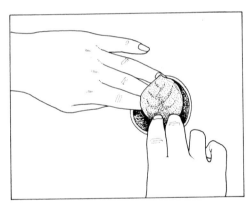

Insert into cutting compost.

The large, colourful leaves of *Begonia rex* will form roots and new plants. There are two methods but for both it is essential to choose a healthy, unblemished leaf nearing the peak of its development. Prepare a half seed tray filled with cutting compost, pressed lightly to give a flat surface, and watered. The first method is to turn the leaf over to expose the large veins on the underside. With a sharp knife, make short cuts across each of the main veins. Place the leaf, the right way up, on to the moist compost and weigh down with small stones here and there, to bring the cut surfaces in contact with the compost. Slip the tray into a polythene bag, knot loosely and stand out of full sun, preferably where there is a source of warmth under the tray. Eventually small plantlets will form from the leaf which, when larger, can be potted up separately. The alternative method involves not cutting the veins but cutting the leaf into large, postage-stamp squares, each containing part of a major vein. These are either laid on to or inserted upright into cutting compost, then kept warm and moist in the same way.

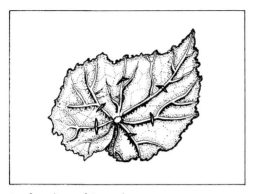

Leaf cuttings of *Begonia rex.*
Cut the main veins on the back of a healthy leaf.

Place the leaf right side up on to moist cutting compost and weight down with a few pebbles.

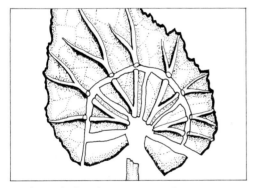

Another method involves cutting triangles, each containing a portion of the junction where the leaves meet the leaf stalk.

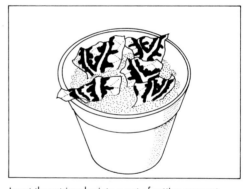

Insert these triangles into a pot of cutting compost.

Begonia masoniana is a little more difficult. The best method is to cut triangular-shaped wedges from the leaf, so that the most pointed angles of each consist of a portion of the cluster of main veins that run into the leaf stalk at the base. These are inserted upright into cutting compost. *Streptocarpus* root easily from leaf cuttings. There are two methods. Leaves can be cut across and the cut ends inserted upright in a compost of equal amounts of peat-based compost and vermiculite. Alternatively, cut the leaf

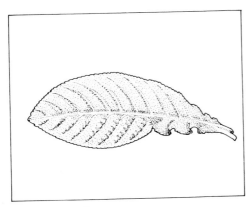

Leaf cuttings of *Streptocarpus.*
Select a healthy leaf.

(a) Turn it over and cut down each side of the midrib, trimming up the ends, or (b) cut across the leaf, making points to denote the bases.

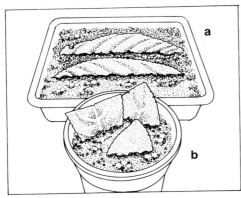

(a) Insert leaf lengths on edge, so that the cut veins are pointing down into the compost. This is where the new plants will grow. (b) Insert leaf sections upright. Roots and new plants will form.

longways along each side of the main vein. Throw the vein away and insert each length with the cut edge downwards into a tray of the same compost. Keep warm and moist. Roots will form at the bottoms of the small veins and plantlets develop which can be potted separately.

STEM SECTIONS

Sections of thick stems of plants like some rhizomatous begonias (*B. manicata* for example), *Dieffenbachia* (dumb cane) and *Dracaena* can be used for propagation. Select healthy, mature stems which have not become woody. Cut sections about 2 inches (5 cm) in length, each preferably containing at least two nodes. Leaves need not be present and can be cut off if they are in the way. Prepare a pot or small tray of moist cutting compost, nestle the stem sections into this so that they are half buried horizontally, cover with polythene or place in a propagating case, keep warm and out of direct sun to root. When shoots develop the new plants can be potted.

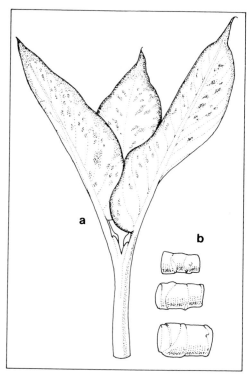

Stem cuttings of *Dieffenbachia.*
Above: If you take a long stem of *Dieffenbachia*, the tip, cut below a node (leaf joint) will make one cutting (a). The remaining stem can be cut into sections containing two nodes (b).

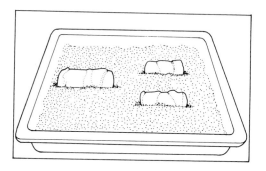

IMPORTANT NOTE

Always wear gloves when handling *Dieffenbachia*, as sap can be an irritant. Never get sap in or near the mouth.

PLANTLETS

Many plants produce smaller versions of themselves on leaves, fronds or runners. These, when large enough to handle, can easily be taken off, pushed into their own small pot of compost and will grow their own roots.

AIR LAYERING

This is a useful technique by which 'cuttings' can be induced to grow roots while still attached to the parent plant. Overgrown rubber plants are the usual patients for this kind of surgery. Of course, one can simply cut off the tips to root as cuttings but air layering ensures a greater chance of success, very important when the old plant is virtually a member of the family. The method described is for a rubber plant but is similar for other plants such as *Monstera* (Swiss cheese plant) and *Fatsia*.

Find a point on the stem, about 12 inches (30 cm) from the shoot tip, where you want

Left: Nestle the stem sections horizontally into cutting compost until half buried.

the roots to grow. Cut off two or three leaves at this point to give access to the stem. (Place newspaper beneath to protect your carpet from the white sap which will fall. This stops quickly and will not harm the plant.) Open the base of a polythene bag and slip the 'sleeve' over the shoot tip until it is below the point where the cut will be made. Secure the sleeve under the position of the cut by tying tightly with string. With a very sharp knife, carefully make an upward-sloping cut towards the tip of the plant. Make this ½ inch (1.25 cm) long and finish so that it is no more than halfway through the stem. The top of the cut should finish just under a node (leaf joint). Wedge the cut open with a sliver of matchstick because this is where the roots will grow from. Pull up the polythene sleeve so that you can pack moist cutting compost (equal parts of peat and sharp sand) around the cut. Bunch the sleeve tightly around this ball and tie tightly above the compost. Rooting will take six to eight weeks. During this

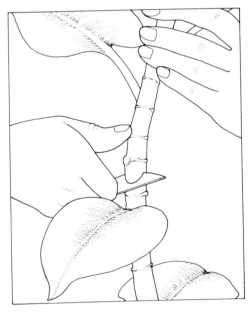

Air layering of a rubber plant.
Begin by removing some leaves 1 to 2 feet (30 to 60 cm) from the shoot tip.

Make an upward slanting cut ½ inch (1.25 cm) long, halfway through the stem. Stop just under a leaf joint.

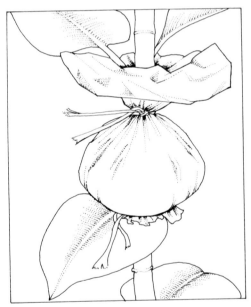

Wedge the cut open with a sliver of matchstick. Pull the polythene bag up round the cut and fill tightly with moist cutting compost.

time you may need to loosen the tie and water the compost inside the polythene. When roots are visible through the poly-thene the rooted layer can be cut from the parent plant, polythene removed and plant potted up.

After a couple of months, roots will have formed and the air layer can be cut from the parent plant and potted up.

Symbols in A–Z of house plants

* Reliable flowering plant. Plants which should flower regularly with little effort on the part of the grower.

☐ Good office plant. However, more tropical, foliage plants will need good humidity. Group them together into large containers for the best effect. Watering problems can be solved by investing in 'self-watering' containers which have an indicator to tell the grower when to top up the reservoir.

Other plants recommended, like cacti and succulents, will do well only if given a bright, windowsill position.

☼ Suitable for a cold, draughty room.

Ⓑ Good plant for a beginner.

● Good plant to try in a dark corner. However, no plant really grows much in a very dark corner. Try to swap them around occasionally so that they do receive some light.

2

ONE HUNDRED
HOUSE PLANTS – AN A TO Z

ACHIMENES

Common name: hot water plant
Position: Good but not direct light. Normal room temperatures of 60 to 70°F (15 to 21°C) are ideal.
Watering: Carefully as the tubercles come into growth, just allowing the surface to dry out between waterings during summer but no water while dormant in winter.
Feeding: Every fortnight with a formula for flowering plants when growing strongly during summer.
Special points: These beautiful flowering plants are related to African violets and share their dislike of water on the leaves, which, particularly in strong light, will scorch them. They will benefit from being given water left to reach room temperature but certainly not the hot water that their common name suggests. Plants are started off between February and April by planting the tubercles which look like anglers' maggots. Place six or seven of these ½ an inch (1.25 cm) under the surface of peat-based

Achimenes

compost in a 4-inch (10-cm) pot. They will need warmth to get them going, so a propagating case is an advantage at this stage. As soon as they appear they need good light to develop. Some staking may be necessary to prevent the stems from flopping over. The exotic-looking flowers are available in many pretty colours, mainly blues and pinks. By the end of summer they will begin to look tired and watering should gradually stop so that by autumn they will have died down. Label the pots, store in a dry place, and you will be amazed at how many tubercles there will be when you sort them out in the following spring. Seed is very fine and should be germinated in a propagating case for best results.

ADIANTUM

Common name: maidenhair fern
Position: Light shade away from bright windows. Cool to normal room temperatures of 55 to 65°F (13 to 18°C) are ideal although temperatures as low as 40°F (5°C) can be tolerated. At high temperatures the air will be too dry. Stand the plant on a tray of moist gravel and mist regularly to increase humidity.
Watering: Keep moist. Never allow the surface to dry out.
Feeding: Liquid feed fortnightly in summer, monthly in winter.
Special points: Many people complain that they cannot grow these ferns. If you are not careful they end up brown and dry in no time. The reasons for this are dry air and dryness at the roots. Newly bought plants are usually pot bound and need almost daily watering in a warm room. You only have to let the compost dry out once or twice and you are well on the way to failure. One solution is to pot the plant on to a larger-sized pot. There will be more moist compost around the roots and less chance of drying out. It is no coincidence that our grandparents grew better maidenhairs than we do. They had much cooler rooms with no central heating causing dry air. Grouping the ferns with other plants or even planting them into a bowl with plants that like the same conditions is another good way of increasing humidity. Both plants and compost continually give off moisture into the air. If the bowl has no drainage, place 2 inches (5 cm) of pebbles in the bottom.

A maidenhair that has deteriorated to a tangle of brown fronds can be resuscitated by cutting the fronds back to the base and

Adiantum capillus-veneris

keeping the roots moist. Provided you act in time, new growth will appear.

Adiantum capillus-veneris is the most commonly grown maidenhair fern.

AECHMEA

Common name: urn plant
Position: Close to a bright window but not exposed to direct sunlight during mid-summer. Normal room temperatures of 60°F (15°C) and above are welcomed with good humidity but lower temperatures down to 50°F (10°C) will be tolerated.
Watering: Be careful not to over-water the roots but keep the 'urn' topped up.
Feeding: Fortnightly during spring and summer, monthly during autumn and winter.
Special points: This plant belongs to a group called bromeliads which includes pineapples and air plants. Many of them make good house plants but *Aechmea fasciata*, with its rosette of wide leaves, banded and speckled with white, is one of the most popular. The flower head, which can last for six months, appears in the urn or funnel formed by the leaves. Blue flowers appear from pink bracts over a period of a month. In its native habitat the nectar from the flowers would attract hummingbirds which pollinate it. These plants grow in niches up in the branches of trees which is why they have adapted their leaves to hold water. They have light root systems and pre-

Aechmea fasciata

fer a peat-based compost with added coarse peat and perlite. They are easy to grow until the flower spike fades, which is the signal that the whole rosette is about to die off. Fortunately offsets are produced which can be cut away and potted up to make new plants. Alternatively, the dying rosette can be cut off to make room for the new ones. The latter might sound easier but you can be left with a lop-sided plant. This can be corrected by knocking the plant out of its pot, shaking off excess compost and repositioning the new growth.

AESCHYNANTHUS *

Common name: lipstick plant
Position: Good but not too much direct light. Near an east-facing window, for

instance. An even temperature of 65°F (18°C) is ideal but plants will tolerate as low as 45°F (7°C) for short periods if fairly dry at the roots. At higher temperatures, or if the plant is close to a radiator, it may be necessary to raise humidity by standing it on a tray of moist gravel. Do not syringe with water as this can damage the leaves.

Watering: Allow the surface of the compost to feel dry between waterings but keep moist when in flower.

Feeding: Weekly in summer but monthly during winter using liquid feed for flowering house plants.

Special points: Having grown these plants in a warm greenhouse I thought they would be difficult in the house. However, I have been growing *Aeschynanthus radicans* (sometimes called *A. longiflorus* or *A.*

Aeschynanthus 'Mona Lisa'

javanicus) indoors with great success. Even when not in flower the plant is attractive, its trailing stems bearing ranks of greyish-green, oval, pointed leaves cascading over the edge of the pot. Plants should flower at least twice a year. The dark-purple calyx appears first and as the red flower bud emerges it really does look like a lipstick. Cuttings of non-flowering shoots 3 inches (7.5 cm) long are best taken in spring or summer (see pp. 14–15). When rooted, plant three to a pot. Sometimes *Aeschynanthus speciosus* is grown which has bright green leaves and flame-coloured flowers.

AGLAONEMA □

Common name: Chinese evergreen

Position: Medium light will keep growth healthy. Keep out of direct light in summer. Normal room temperatures of 60 to 70°F (15 to 21°C) are appreciated. Although they will survive temperatures as low as 50°F (10°C) if kept on the dry side, they dislike fluctuations.

Watering: Keep moist but allow the surface of the compost to feel dry between waterings, particularly during winter.

Feeding: Weekly during summer and monthly during winter with a liquid feed for foliage house plants.

Special points: This is not a plant which will attract immediate attention but it makes an admirable display of foliage. There are

Aglaonema 'Silver Queen'

with other plants. Propagation is by dividing the clump into separate stems, taking cuttings of the shoot tips or stem sections (see pp. 20–1).

ANTHURIUM * □

Common name: flamingo flower
Position: Good but not direct light. A constant room temperature of 60 to 65°F (15 to 18°C) is ideal.
Watering: Allow the surface of the compost to feel dry between waterings. Never let plants stand in water.
Feeding: Liquid feed fortnightly in summer, monthly during winter with a formula for flowering house plants.
Special points: These will take up plenty of space when they become mature but

several different kinds with leaves of grey, cream and shades of green. *Aglaonema 'Silver Queen'* is the most common and will make a good clump with leaves 12 inches (30 cm) high. Although these plants will tolerate low light they will not thrive if placed in a permanently gloomy corner. Likewise, although they can tolerate a temperature of 50°F (10°C) they will not respond well if this fluctuates up to 70°F (21°C) and back regularly. Brown tips on the leaves is an indication of dry air and the plant should benefit from misting, standing on a tray of moist pebbles, or being grouped

Anthurium scherzerianum

reward proper care with almost continuous flower if given sufficient light and plant food. My own plant takes up one end of a sideboard in an east-facing room opposite the window. Both foliage and flowers are very handsome. *Anthurium scherzerianum* from Costa Rica is probably the most commonly seen. The part that looks like a petal is the large waxy red spathe from the top of which the twisted spadix spirals out. This is the part that actually bears the tiny true flowers. *Anthurium andreanum* from Colombia is similar but has a straight spadix and more heart-shaped spathe. There are varieties with white or pink spathes.

If you can picture these wonderful plants growing up in the trees in their warm, humid tropical rain forests then you can imagine the sort of conditions they might enjoy in the home. Avoid fluctuations in temperature which can cause stop-start growth resulting in deformed leaves. Another problem is brown leaf tips caused by dry air, preventable by standing the plant on a wide saucer of moist gravel to increase humidity.

There is a species grown for its beautiful, large, heart-shaped leaves which are a shimmering dark green overlaid with silvery veins. *Anthurium crystallinum*, the crystal anthurium, is not an easy plant to grow in the house. I have never been able to provide sufficient heat and humidity for it to thrive. If you like a challenge, though, this might be for you. All these plants can be propagated by division.

ASPARAGUS ☐ ☼ Ⓑ

Common name: asparagus fern
Position: Good but not direct light but can tolerate some shade. Normal room temperatures of 60 to 65°F (15 to 18°C) are appreciated but they can also tolerate temperatures as low as 40 to 50°F (5 to 10°C).
Watering: During periods of strong growth keep well watered but allow the surface of the soil to dry out between waterings during winter.
Feeding: Weekly during summer, monthly during winter with a formula for foliage house plants.

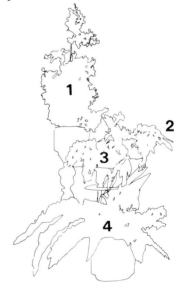

1 *Asparagus myriocladus*
2 *A. plumosus* 'Nanus'
3 *A. densiflorus* 'Sprengeri'
4 *A. densiflorus* 'Myers'

Special points: Although always referred to as 'ferns' these are flowering plants in the same family as lilies. They will bear insignificant flowers, sometimes followed by berries. True ferns, of course, are spore-bearing and have no flowers at all. True ferns need moist conditions and suffer as soon as their roots become even slightly dry. Asparagus, however, have tuberous storage roots that enable them to withstand short droughts. I have a busy friend who has admitted to not having watered her plants for six weeks at a time and they have always survived. This, of course, is not the proper treatment for our plants to thrive on but it does make them excellent candidates for beginners. *A. plumosus* 'Nanus' from South Africa is the familiar accompaniment to carnation buttonholes. *A. densiflorus* 'Sprengeri' is the next well known, with its wispy trailing stems. There are three more worth knowing. *A. densiflorus* 'Myers' has stems like bushy tails up to 3 feet (1 metre) long, *A. myriocladus* is tall, elegant and oriental-looking, and *A. falcatus* is the sicklethorn with larger, flatter, modified leaves. Watch out when handling these as they can all have nasty hidden thorns.

Plants are easy to raise by seed which is large and hard. Soak overnight before sowing during late spring or early summer. Mature plants can be divided. This is not easy as the roots often make a solid mass. The plants are so tough that the roots can be sliced or even sawn apart.

ASPIDISTRA

Common name: cast-iron plant
Position: Medium but not direct light is preferred but will tolerate low light. They will thrive in warm rooms of 60 to 70°F (15 to 21°C) but can also tolerate temperatures close to freezing point. I know a gardener in London who has successfully grown them in a sheltered spot outside.

Aspidistra elatior (right) and *A. e.* 'Variegata' (left)

Watering: Allow soil surface to dry out between waterings.

Feeding: Fortnightly during summer and monthly during winter with a feed for foliage house plants.

Special points: This plant earned its tough-sounding name during Victorian times when it enjoyed great popularity and seemed well able to withstand gas fumes, dust and cool temperatures. If the Victorians liked their aspidistras then the reverse was also true. These plants grew into large clumps untroubled by the dry air of central heating which can cause ugly brown tips to the leaves and encourage spider mite. If your plant seems sickly and has a speckled, dried-out look about it, then examine closely for this pest (see pp. 122–3). Growth begins in the spring when several new leaves push up from beneath the compost. More water and feed will be needed at this time. During summer strange, dark flowers sometimes appear at the soil surface which in the wild would be pollinated by slugs. *Aspidistra elatior* is the most commonly grown and its handsome variegated form is well worth hunting for. Propagation is by division best carried out in spring or early summer.

ASPLENIUM B

Common name: bird's nest fern

Position: Medium light away from direct sunlight which scorches the fronds. Normal room temperatures of 60 to 70°F (15 to 21°C) suit them well. Avoid fluctuations which cause deformities by making the fronds unfurl at an uneven rate.

Watering: Keep moist but do not leave standing in water.

Feeding: Use a liquid feed for foliage house plants fortnightly during summer but only a couple of times during winter.

Special points: *Asplenium nidus* from tropical Asia and Australia is the most commonly grown. Wide, bright green shiny fronds unfurl from the centre of the plant which is dark, fibrous and reminiscent of a bird's nest. They will become very dusty and need to be cleaned regularly with a soft,

Right: *Asplenium nidus*

dry cloth. These ferns can live for several years in the same pot without being disturbed. Eventually the plant begins to look tired, which is the signal to pot on into a larger pot and fresh house plant compost. Propagation by spores is not easy indoors (see p. 13) but tiny plants are often offered for sale.

Asplenium bulbiferum is different in appearance, more difficult to find for sale, yet very easy to grow. The dainty, divided fronds bear bulbils or baby ferns as they grow older giving rise to the common names of mother spleenwort and hen and chicken. These bulbils can be pulled off, inserted into fresh compost and grown on into new plants. A very good fern for a cold room.

Begonia X elatior

BEGONIA ☼ B

Position: Good light is needed for all types. Flowering kinds need some direct light every day. Normal room temperatures suit them well but most can tolerate lower temperatures down to 45 to 50°F (7 to 10°C).

Watering: Always allow the surface of the compost to dry out slightly between waterings.

Feedings: Fortnightly during summer, monthly during winter. Flowering begonias should be given a high-potash formula.

Special points: There are basically three different types of begonias. Those with fibrous roots include *B. semperflorens*, more

Begonia 'Corallina de Lucerna'

Begonia rex

often grown as a bedding plant. Potted up and grown near a sunny window they also make a cheap, colourful house plant. *Begonia* × *elatior* has become very popular recently for its compact shape and profuse double flowers available in many colours. Both of these eventually become straggly but cut them down very hard to within 2 inches (5 cm) of the base and, provided they are in good light, they will grow back again. There are many fibrous-rooted species, the most popular of which is a tall 'cane' begonia with long stems, large, tapering, spotted leaves and clusters of pink flowers. *Begonia* 'Corallina de Lucerna' was bred, not surprisingly, in Switzerland. I call it the 'spotty begonia' and find it almost indestructible. In poor light it makes a good foliage plant, it flowers well in good light and tolerates

heavy pruning. Cuttings of shoots 3 to 4 inches (7.5 to 10 cm) long root easily and can be tried in water as well as compost (see page 17).

Rhizomatous begonias, like *B. rex* and *B. masoniana* (the Iron Cross begonia), have thick fleshy stems that lie on top of the compost. There are more uncommon rhizomatous species and also hybrids, like *B.* × 'Cleopatra' and *B.* 'Tiger', which have small, delicately shaped, dense leaves from a creeping stem. Grown mainly for their foliage, most of this group, notably *B. rex* and *B. masoniana*, can be propagated by leaf cuttings (see pp. 18–19) or by cutting 1- to 2-inch (2.5- to 5-cm) sections of rhizome, nestling them into the surface of cutting compost where they will root and sprout new shoots and leaves. This group needs careful watering as the roots easily suffer if too wet. Hairy, large-leaved types like *B. rex* have to be cleaned with a soft brush.

Tuberous begonias can be grown indoors. Start the tubers off in February or March by planting them concave side upwards into a tray of moist peat with the tops of the tubers above the surface. When they have begun to root and sprout shoots, pot them carefully into 4-inch (10-cm) pots. They will need very good light to do well. If the plants outgrow their pots before coming into flower then pot on into 6-inch (15-cm) pots. After the summer they will die down. Gradually dry them off and store dry in their pots at 55°F (13°C) until the following spring.

BELOPERONE *

Common name: shrimp plant
Position: Some direct light will ensure continuous flowering. I keep my plants near an east-facing window. A temperature of 55 to 65°F (13 to 18°C) suits them well, although temperatures as low as 40°F (5°C) can be tolerated.
Watering: Allow the surface to dry out slightly between waterings.
Feeding: Weekly during summer and monthly during winter with a formula for flowering house plants.
Special points: *Beloperone guttata* earns its common name on account of the shrimp-coloured bracts from which the small, white tuberous flowers emerge like shrimp tails. If your plant does not flower continuously

Beloperone guttata

then you must be doing something wrong. Should the plant become too large, prune hard in spring, cutting the stems just above a leaf or nodal swelling on the stem. If you have plenty of room, pot the plant on regularly until you have a very grand shrubby specimen covered in flowers. Cuttings 3 inches (7.5 cm) long root easily. If there is no non-flowering material, pinch the flowers and buds off the cutting. Plant three small plants into a large shallow clay pot for instant effect, greater control over watering, and increased humidity.

BOUGAINVILLEA

Common name: paper flowers
Position: To flower well they must have good direct light during active growth periods. As well as normal room temperatures of 60 to 65°F (15 to 18°C), temperatures almost down to freezing point can be tolerated if plants are allowed to go dormant and are kept dry at the roots.
Watering: While producing leaves and flowers water well, just allowing the surface to dry out in between. While resting during winter keep very much on the dry side, especially at low temperatures.
Feeding: When the plant has begun growing strongly and you can imagine the root growth has speeded up in spring, feed fortnightly with a liquid feed for flowering house plants. As plants ease up during autumn stop feeding altogether.

Bougainvillea 'Alexandra'

Special points: For an exotic-looking plant associated with trips abroad to sunnier climates, the bougainvillea is surprisingly tough. As a house plant it can be disappointing unless you have a very bright spot for it. A sun lounge or porch would be ideal. At cold winter temperatures leaves may drop but the plant will stay healthy and ready to burst back into growth in spring. If you need to keep your plant within bounds, prune back last year's stems to within a few buds of the older wood in February. I also move my plants into a very warm position at this time, which gives a quick boost to new

stems and flowers. The showy, 'papery' parts are bracts. True flowers appear in the centre of these. If you are adventurous there are not only pink and red varieties but shades of orange and white. Propagate by taking shoot-tip cuttings 3 inches (7.5 cm) long in spring.

BULBS (DAFFODILS, TULIPS AND HYACINTHS)

Position: For bulbs in bowls and pots a good light position in a cool room will give the longest colour on the most compact plants. A dark, warm position results in leggy, short-lived plants.

Watering: Never allow the bulb fibre or compost to dry out, but do not waterlog.

Feeding: Not necessary.

Special points: It is great fun to buy bulbs (and corms) which would naturally flower in spring and force them to flower in winter. These are planted in autumn, starting with hyacinths. Always buy prepared hyacinths if you want them to flower before Christmas and remember to plant before mid-September. Daffodils and tulips come in all sorts of colours and sizes. Dwarf types are obviously more accommodating, otherwise much staking and tying will be required. There will be quite a long period between planting and flowering with all except 'Paperwhite' narcissi which need only six weeks to come into flower.

Hyacinths are usually planted into bowls.

Spring flowering bulbs

As there is no drainage hole, bulb fibre must be used. I favour planting them in boxes or individual pots of ordinary potting compost, arranging them into bowls as they come into bud. Leave the top or 'nose' of the bulb protruding. Larger, deeper pots will be needed for daffodils and tulips. The tips of these should be just above the surface. As daffodil bulbs are so large it is possible to have almost two layers in the pot but staggered so that the lower bulbs can grow upwards unrestricted. Having watered them in, the best place for the bulbs is under a good layer of soil or peat in the garden where they will remain, cold and dark, until the roots are well formed. When the shoots are 2 to 3 inches (5 to 7.5 cm) high they can be brought indoors. If you have no garden then any cool, preferably dark place will do.

CACTI □ ☼

Position: Desert cacti need good direct light and must be on a bright windowsill to grow and flower well. A cool position in the house is best so that they stop growing completely during winter. The west-facing windowsill of an unheated bedroom proves ideal for my collection.

Watering: Between March and October they should be watered almost as much as any other house plant. Allow the surface of the compost to become dry between waterings. Failure to water regularly might not result in death but in a very sad, neglected cactus. During winter, water maybe two or three times in a temperature of 55 to 60°F (13 to 15°C) to prevent shrivelling.

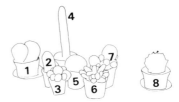

1 *Mammillaria karwinskiana*
2 *Cephalocereus senilis*
3 *Mammillaria zeilmanniana*
4 *Weberbauerocereus johnstonii*
5 *Notocactus magnificus*
6 *Mammillaria elongata*
7 *Mammillaria bombycina*
8 *Ferocactus haematacanthus*

More might be needed at higher temperatures, none at all at lower temperatures.

Feeding: Between March and October feed monthly with a special cactus fertiliser which is formulated to encourage the right sort of growth and flowering. No feeding in winter.

Special points: Cacti need a well-drained compost. Should repotting be necessary, do this in late spring, supporting the plant with a collar of newspaper or thick cloth. I use a compost of three parts peat (equal amounts of moss and sedge) to one part of sharp sand or grit with enough John Innes fertiliser to make a No. 1 strength. Special cactus compost is good or you could try adding extra peat and grit to a John Innes No. 2.

CALATHEA

Common name: peacock plant
Position: Good light is necessary for healthy growth but too much direct light will scorch leaves. A north, east or slightly shaded window is best. Warm temperatures of between 60 and 70°F (15 to 21°C) are required for plants to do well though temperatures down to 50°F (10°C) can be tolerated in emergencies.
Watering: Keep the compost moist in temperatures of 65°F (18°C) and above. Below this allow the surface to dry out slightly between waterings.

Right: Calathea veitchiana

Feeding: Fortnightly during summer but monthly during winter with a formula for foliage house plants.

Special points: A varied group containing many species grown for their foliage. They vary from compact, rounded clumps to long, graceful specimens several feet high. With their origins in tropical South America and the West Indies it is not surprising that they thrive in warm, constant temperatures and high humidity. The warmth we can easily achieve but the humidity is more difficult. Dry air results in poor growth and brown tips to the leaves. Spider mite, to which these are particularly prone (see pp. 122-3), are also encouraged by dry air. The effort of misting regularly and providing a wide tray of moist pebbles will be worthwhile. Propagation is by dividing the clumps.

CALLISIA ☼ B

Common name: Sometimes shares the name wandering Jew with *Tradescantia*, a very close relative. Has earned the name 'Terry Wogan Plant' by appearing on his show.

Position: Good light is necessary for healthy, compact growth. This should include some direct light in winter. Move away from a very bright window during summer to prevent scorching. A warm room is acceptable but cooler conditions of 55 to 60°F (13 to 15°C) are preferred and lower temperatures down to 45°F (7°C) are tolerated.

Watering: Keep moist in summer but allow the surface of the compost to dry out between waterings during winter.

Special points: Not a wildly exciting

Callisia repens

house plant but makes a compact mound of foliage. Many branching, slender stems arch out from the middle crowded with small, closely packed apple-green leaves. After a while the stems grow rather straggly. Cut them back hard and provided the plant is in good light new shoots will grow. Tips of shoots 2 inches (5 cm) long root easily. I usually insert four into a 3-inch (7.5-cm) pot of compost. When they have rooted, just pinching out the tips will encourage them to start branching. Cuttings also root well in water (see p. 17). Flowers are often produced but are so insignificant that they go largely unnoticed. Good plant for a bright bathroom windowsill or shelf.

CEROPEGIA ✱ ☐ ☼ B

Common name: rosary plant, string of hearts

Position: Prefers good, direct sunlight to do well. However, I have seen a handsome specimen some distance from a small window which did very well apart from having larger spaces between the leaves. Normal room temperatures between 60 and 70°F (15 and 21°C) are acceptable but much lower temperatures down to 40°F (5°C) can be tolerated, making this an excellent choice for a porch.

Watering: Always allow the surface of the compost to dry out between waterings. During winter, when growth is less active, less water is needed but in a hot, dry

Ceropegia woodii

bobbles which are tubers on the stems like beads on a rosary. These can be removed and nestled into the surface of some very gritty cutting compost. The trick with getting these tubers to root is to keep them very dry, allowing the compost to dry out almost completely before watering again. If your plant has not produced any of these tubers then stem tip cuttings 2 to 3 inches (5 to 7.5 cm) long can be used instead. I have chosen an unusual container for my plant – a tall, rather primitive earthenware pot. The bottom third was filled with expanded clay pebbles before I potted the ceropegia into a very well-drained compost similar to that used for cacti (see p. 40). The trailing stems are now almost 5 feet (150 cm) long. The plant lives on a shelf about 5 feet (150 cm) from an east-facing window. Unusual, small flowers are produced down the stems which look like tiny purplish coronets. *Ceropegia* is in the same plant family as *Hoya* and *Stephanotis*.

atmosphere do not let the plant shrivel up.
Feeding: Fortnightly during summer but no feed at all during winter.
Special points: *Ceropegia woodii* earns its common names well. Thin, purplish stems grow out of a small tuber which lies at the surface of the compost. From the stems grow pairs of prettily mottled heart-shaped leaves. Also, at intervals, appear woody

CHAMAEDOREA ☼ B

Common name: parlour palm
Position: Bright light is needed for healthy growth. During summer, direct light can scorch the leaves but in winter a dreary corner will result in thin, poor growth. My plant lives to the side of a west-facing window during summer but I move it closer to the light during winter. Normal room temperatures of 60 to 70°F (15 to 21°C)

are ideal but temperatures down to 50°F (10°C) can be tolerated.

Watering: Allow the surface of the compost to just begin to feel dry before watering again.

Feeding: Fortnightly during summer but only monthly during winter with a formula for foliage house plants.

Special points: *Chamaedorea elegans* is indeed an elegant little palm. Not everybody wants to find the space for larger palms but like their leafy, exotic effect. The parlour

palm will only reach about 3 feet (1 metre) in height and will grow very slowly. Plants should last for many years but, although they are tough, can have problems. After three to four years in the same pot they might produce stunted-looking, yellowish leaves which no amount of feeding will correct. The cure is to repot during spring or summer. A scorched look to the leaves might be caused by spider mite (see pp. 122–3). Brown tips and spider mite are encouraged by dry air, so raise the humidity by standing the plant on a tray of moist pebbles and mist regularly. Dust and then wipe leaves to keep them clean.

CHLOROPHYTUM ☼ B

Common name: spider plant

Position: Needs good light but direct light in summer will scorch the leaves. Normal warm room temperatures are acceptable but above 65°F (18°C) dry air can scorch leaf tips. Lower temperatures down to 40°F (5°C) are happily tolerated.

Watering: Keep these plants moist during periods of active growth but if the room temperature drops during winter, allow the surface of the compost to dry out between waterings. Never leave standing in water.

Feeding: Fortnightly during summer and winter if the plant is in good winter light and at warm room temperatures. No feed at low temperatures.

Special points: *Chlorophytum comosum*

Chamaedorea elegans

varieties are those most commonly grown as house plants and they are very common. Even people who say they know nothing about house plants can recognise a spider plant. Nevertheless, these natives of South Africa should not be derided by house plant snobs because well grown, they can make magnificent specimens. To achieve this, good light is crucial, as is regular feeding and not allowing the plant to become pot-bound until it reaches its final pot size. Long stems will appear from the centres of the 'spider', which bear small white flowers followed by plantlets. On large specimens the plantlets hang down around the mother plant in an impressive mass. The main problem I am asked to solve is that of leaves turning brown at the tips. This is caused by hot, dry air. During winter it might be a good idea to move them out of a centrally heated room into a cooler one. If this proves to be impossible then grouping them with other plants, misting and arranging them on trays of moist pebbles will all help. Propagation is very easy and consists of simply removing plantlets, which have often already begun to root, and tucking them into small pots of compost. These are excellent plants for hanging baskets or stands.

Left: *Chlorophytum comosum* 'Vittatum'

Right: *Cissus rhombifolia* 'Ellen Danica'

CISSUS □ ☼ Ⓑ ●

Common name: kangaroo vine/grape ivy
Position: Requires good light to do well but can tolerate some shade. Avoid direct sunlight which can cause scorching and yellowing of leaves. Temperatures of 60 to 70°F (15 to 20°C) are ideal but as low as 40°F (5°C) can be tolerated.
Watering: Keep moist but allow the surface to dry out between waterings.
Feeding: Liquid feed fortnightly during summer. In winter feed monthly at higher temperatures but not at all if kept cool.
Special points: *Cissus antarctica*, as the common name kangaroo vine implies, comes from Australia. A tough house plant, it was

once widely grown as a vigorous foliage climber. An easy plant, it can become yellow-leaved and straggly if proper care is not received. Pay attention to regular summer feeding and prune back in spring to promote fresh growth which hides woody stems. Propagation is by tip cuttings 4 inches (10 cm) long. These days, *Cissus rhombifolia*, which used to be called *Rhoicissus rhomboidea* or grape ivy, is more common, particularly the variety 'Ellen Danica'. Unfortunately this, though attractive, can be prone to mildew. Never allow the plant to dry out at the roots as this encourages the problem. An excellent group of plants for covering an inside screen or trellis. *Cissus discolor* is sometimes grown but is more difficult and needs higher temperatures and humidity. The heart-shaped, silver-marked leaves with bright maroon undersides are very attractive.

Citrus (right *Fortunella margarita* 'Variegata', left X *Citrofortunella mitis*)

CITRUS

Position: Good light is essential. Place near a window so that some direct sunlight is received every day. Temperatures as low as 40°F (5°C) will happily be tolerated during winter but very little growth will take place. This makes them ideal for a porch. Normal room temperatures are appreciated but at 60°F (15°C) and above, increase humidity by misting and standing the pot on a gravel tray.

Watering: Keep moist during spring and summer but in winter, particularly at lower temperatures, allow the surface to become dry between waterings.

Feeding: Fortnightly in summer with a feed formulated for flowering and fruiting plants, like a tomato fertiliser. Reduce to monthly during winter, unless the temperature drops below 60°F (15°C), in which case stop altogether.

Special points: Citrus make delightful house plants with the possibility of edible fruit as well as attractive, shiny leaves and pretty, perfumed, white flowers. There are many kinds to choose from. I have just bought a 'Myers Lemon' and 'Valencia Orange' already covered in flower buds so that I know I am off to a good start. It can be fun to grow your own citrus from pips taken from oranges, limes, grapefruit, kumquats etc. as long as you realise that you might have to wait many years for flowers and fruit to form. To sow, fill a pot with seed compost, push the pips in so that they are buried by ¼ inch (½ cm), cover with polythene and place somewhere warm (an airing cupboard will do). As soon as they germinate (which takes two to three weeks), uncover and place on a light windowsill. Sometimes more than one seedling will emerge from each pip. Grow all these as two should be identical to the parent plant which means they stand a better chance of fruiting. Pot on into a bigger pot annually until you run out of space. Citrus respond well to pruning which is best done in spring to retain a good shape. Old, misshapen plants can be cut right back into woody old stems with a good chance of promoting new growth. Stem tip cuttings root easily given warmth and moisture. If you only have room for small plants there are kumquats which, strictly speaking, fall under the genus *Fortunella* and the pretty calamondin, correctly known as *Citrofortunella mitis*. This flowers and produces small (just over 1 inch (2.5 cm) in diameter) orange fruits all year round. Be on the look-out for scale insect and mealy bug (see pp. 123-4).

CLIVIA ✳ ✿ Ⓑ

Common name: kaffir lily
Position: Good light is necessary for reliable flowering. However, do not expose to harsh sunlight during midsummer. My plant does well in an east-facing window. An ideal winter temperature is 55 to 60°F (13 to 15°C). A very hot room would not suit them. Lower temperatures of 35 to 40°F (2 to 5°C) will be tolerated.

Watering: Just allow the surface of the compost to dry out between waterings.

Feeding: Use a formula for flowering house plants fortnightly during spring and summer but just a couple of times during winter if kept at higher temperatures.

Special points: To ensure the production of a flower spike each year, it is vital to give good light and to feed and water well during spring and summer. Though expensive to buy, I think they are well worth it for their bright, orange, trumpet-shaped flowers. Do not pot them on until the roots are bulging in the pot (maybe every four to five years) as they flower best undisturbed. After

Clivia miniata

flowering, fruits are often produced which take a year to ripen. When they are red and soft, take the large seeds out and plant them, covering with about ¼ inch (½ cm) of compost. Keep warm and moist and small plants will grow which could be flowering in four years' time. This might seem a long wait but my mother was patient and is now rewarded with five fine flowering plants it would cost her an arm and a leg to buy. The only other way to increase stock is to wait until the plant has grown into a clump, when it can be divided.

COCOS

Common name: coconut palm
Position: Good but not direct light. Warm room temperatures of 60 to 70°F (15 to 21°C) plus are needed for healthy growth.
Watering: Allow the surface to dry out between waterings.
Feeding: Fortnightly during summer and monthly during winter with a well-balanced house plant fertiliser.
Special points: Bearing in mind that these are seedlings of the huge coconut palm, *Cocos nucifera*, they are not at all easy to keep healthy for any length of time. Watering is often difficult because there is not enough space in the top of the pot. Either stand in water for an hour to soak up from below or carefully pot on into a larger pot

without disturbing the roots or altering the height of the nut in the compost which should have sharp sand added for good drainage. Keep a constant look-out for spider mites, which love these plants (see pp. 122–3).

Right: *Cocos nucifera*

CODIAEUM □

Common name: croton, Joseph's coat

Position: Good, direct light. Place near a window but not a south-facing windowsill during summer. Thrives in temperatures of 60 to 70°F (15 to 21°C) and can go down to 55°F (13°C) but avoid fluctuations.

Watering: Keep the compost moist but not saturated. At lower temperatures, let it become a little drier between waterings.

Feeding: Fortnightly during summer with a feed for foliage house plants. Stop feeding for the winter.

Special points: Bright, showy foliage house plants, there are lots of differently coloured and shaped leaf types to choose from. The broad-leaved kinds need to be dusted and wiped regularly to keep dust off the sur-

faces. Falling leaves can be caused by too dark a position, fluctuations in temperature, or a draught. Leaves scorching at the tips could mean the plant is too near a radiator and needs more humidity. After a while plants can grow tall and leggy. Rather than throw them away, try cutting hard back to within 6 inches (15 cm) of the base during spring. Given good light, new shoots should grow and the old one can be used as a tip cutting.

COFFEA

Common name: coffee plant

Position: Good but not direct light. My plant does well ten feet away from an east-facing window. They like warmth but not accompanied by dry air.

Above: *Codiaeum*

Right: *Coffea arabica*

Watering: Keep moist during spring and summer but dry out a little more between waterings during winter.

Feeding: Fortnightly liquid feeds during summer but only a couple of times during winter.

Special points: The Arabian coffee plant (*Coffea arabica*) makes an attractive specimen but with its love of warmth and humidity is not easy to grow without ugly brown tips to the leaves. If heat is accompanied by dry air, settle for a gentler warmth of 60°F (15°C) and increase humidity by using a gravel tray and by misting regularly. Large plants in the more even light of a conservatory might eventually flower. Red, berry-like fruits are produced, each containing two seeds which are the coffee beans of commerce. As cuttings are slow to root, the best way to produce your own plants is to buy and sow seed.

Coleus

COLEUS

Common name: flame nettle, though I have never heard anybody use it.

Position: Bright light, a sunny windowsill is excellent. These like a warm 60 to 65°F (15 to 18°C) and will not grow well if the temperature dips down below 55°F (13°C) too often.

Watering: They need a lot of water when growing strongly in summer. Should temperatures drop, they are very prone to over-watering and the surface should just begin to dry out in between.

Feeding: Weekly during summer if they are healthy and strong, but only once or twice during winter.

Special points: The worst thing you can do to a coleus is deprive it of light, when it will become sick and spindly. Never leave them sitting in water. A certain amount of leaf-dropping will occur as autumn turns to winter, but young plants should settle down if temperatures are warm enough. As plants grow, pinch the growing tips out regularly to encourage branching and prevent insignificant flowers forming to the detriment of the foliage. Cuttings root very easily and can even be struck in water (see p. 17).

COLUMNEA ✳ Ⓑ

Common name: goldfish plant

Position: These need good light to develop flower buds. Mine thrives close to an east-facing window where light is not too harsh. Constancy of temperature is more important than great heat. A steady 60°F (15°C) during winter should ensure good results. Humidity is important, so keep away from radiators. My plant is surrounded by other house plants which means they all benefit from the moisture given off from leaves and compost. A lone plant should be stood on a tray of moist gravel.

Watering: Keep moist, especially between spring and autumn. During winter the surface of the compost can become dry between waterings.

Feeding: Liquid feed, with a formula for flowering house plants, every fortnight dur-

Columnea 'Stavanger'

Columnea 'Krakatoa'

ing summer but once a month during winter.

Special points: These beautiful trailing house plants are not as difficult to grow as they look. Most are sold in hanging baskets and I think here lie many of the problems. When these are hung up in the house, the small saucer fixed to the bottom to catch drips is not adequate. If you water thoroughly, as you should, water will cascade on to the carpet. As a result, I fear some plants are never given sufficient water, roots die back and the plant gives up and dies. I find it better to stand the container in a large saucer and let the long stems trail over a table, windowsill or mantelpiece. There are several species available but most plants sold are hybrids. These seem to change every year, coming on to the market in spring. This year *Columnea* 'Krakatoa', which has quite a stiff habit and a profusion of bright orange-red flowers which look just like leaping goldfish, seems to be favourite. The stems eventually trail down. For a real trailer, choose *C. microphylla* or *C.* 'Stavanger'. These plants are in the same family as African violets and share their dislike of cold water sprayed on leaves, which can cause ugly marks. If, after a while, they become straggly, prune them back hard after flowering, some time during the summer. Three-inch (7-cm) long cuttings will root easily during spring and summer.

CORDYLINE

Common name: good luck or ti plant
Position: Good but not direct light. Winter temperatures of 60 to 70°F (15 to 21°C) are ideal.
Watering: Allow the surface of the compost to dry out between waterings, especially during winter. Never leave plants standing in water.
Feeding: Fortnightly during summer with a liquid feed for foliage plants. Once a month during winter is plenty.
Special points: The Polynesians grow

Cordyline terminalis

their ti plants (*Cordyline terminalis*) close to their homes as they are thought to bring good luck, hence the name. Foliage plants, grown for their vividly red- and green-coloured leaves, there are several named forms available. Brown tips to the leaves are a sign of general unhappiness caused by insufficient light, low temperatures, or dry air. Keep the leaves clean by dusting regularly and wiping with a moist cloth. There are several ways of propagating these plants. On tall plants the tip can be removed and used as a cutting. Two-inch (5-cm) long, bare sections of stem will root if nestled upright or horizontally into cutting compost and kept warm and moist. Best of all are the 'toe' cuttings. Remove a mature plant from its pot and look at the base. Poking around in the compost there, should reveal one or more stumpy roots. Cut 1-inch (2.5-cm) long pieces away and place them horizontally just under the surface of some potting compost. These will grow smaller roots and also one or more shoots which make the new plant. There are other kinds of cordyline (*C. australis* and *C. indivisa*) but owing to their size and love of lower temperatures they are not very suitable as house plants.

CRASSULA ☐ ☼ B

Common name: money tree, jade tree
Position: as light as possible, otherwise growth will be slow and spindly. Temperatures between 45 and 55°F (7 and 13°C) during winter are ideal. Lower temperatures can be tolerated, down to 35°F (2°C) but at high temperatures during winter poor growth is made.
Watering: Keep moist between March and October but only water sufficiently during winter to prevent shrivelling.
Feeding: Fortnightly during summer with a formula for cacti and succulents. Do not give any feed during the winter rest period.
Special points: The succulent green leaves of *Crassula argentea* give rise to the name of jade plant. It is said that by rubbing the leaves you are brought financial luck, hence money plant. This is a very popular

Crassula argentea

succulent which grows into the shape of a miniature tree. Given plenty of light, plants will produce masses of small, star-shaped, pinkish-white flowers at the ends of shoots. When repotting, use a cactus compost (see p. 40). Propagation can be by taking the shoot tips as cuttings. Leaves will root at the base if inserted into cutting compost.

CRYPTANTHUS ☐

Common name: earth star
Position: Good, bright light is preferred. Room temperatures between 60 and 70°F (15 to 21°C) are ideal but they can tolerate occasional temperature drops to as low as 40°F (5°C) provided the compost is not

too wet. Originating from tropical, steamy places one would think humidity would be a priority. However, I kept a very healthy plant of *Cryptanthus bivittatus* on a bathroom windowsill only a few inches from a radiator with no ill effects. Should plants look scorched, however, stand on trays of moist gravel.

Watering: Definitely not to be overdone. Allow the top few inches of compost to dry out before watering again.

Feeding: Monthly during summer but only a couple of times during winter. As heavy watering is not appreciated, use a foliar feed.

Special points: *Cryptanthus* belong to the bromeliad family which contains air plants, urn plants, and pineapples. In their native habitat these strange but attractive plants would stretch out over rocks and tree stumps rather like terrestrial starfish. As

Cryptanthus (left C. bivittatus, *right* C. bromelioides *'Tricolor')*

they are not accustomed to growing in much soil, but in light leaf litter, a dense compost is not appreciated. Some coarse peat and vermiculite can be added to an ordinary peat compost to keep the texture open. This is also why you have to be so careful with the watering. There are different leaf patterns to choose from, some with long stripes down the leaf, others attractively barred with purple over a greyish-green leaf. *Cryptanthus* 'It' is, perhaps, one of the showiest but *C. bromelioides* 'Tricolor' is a close contender. Rosettes of growth will produce small white flowers in good light. Then the plant will begin to die. However, offsets are produced which form a clump and take over. These can be cut or pulled away and potted up to make new plants.

CTENANTHE

Common name: never never plant
Position: Good but not direct light. Temperatures between 60 and 70°F (15 to 21°C) are ideal and should not drop below 55°F (13°C) for any length of time.
Watering: Keep moist during active growth in summer but be very careful in winter, allowing the top half of the compost to dry out.
Feeding: Fortnightly in summer but only a couple of times during winter with a formula for foliage house plants.
Special points: There are several different species of Ctenanthe to choose from, all

Ctenanthe oppenheimiana

CYCAS ☼

Common name: sago palm

Position: Good light is needed, particularly when the new leaves are forming. Normal room temperatures of between 60 and 70°F (15 to 21°C) are ideal but plants can grow at lower temperatures if required. My plant lives in an unheated porch most of the year with temperatures going down to 40°F (5°C), sometimes lower. During winter I bring the plant into a warm sitting-room to avoid freezing.

Watering: Allow the surface to dry out between waterings.

Feeding: Every month with a well-balanced liquid feed during spring, summer and autumn. No feed during winter.

Special points: *Cycas revoluta* from Japan is the species grown as a house plant. These plants resemble palms but are in an ancient plant group of their own, more closely related to conifers than anything else. Similar plants were probably around when dinosaurs roamed the earth. Plants are expensive to buy but will last for years. They have great character and will often sulk for long periods during which no growth takes place. Keep such plants in good light and make sure the compost does not dry out completely. After a while, one spring or late summer, a whole furl of new leaves will appear at the centre of the plant. This is the time when the plant needs good, all-round light. A porch or greenhouse is ideal. In a

with attractively patterned leaves. *C. oppenheimiana* is one of the more elegant, with very long leaf stalks. These tropical plants are susceptible to dry air and will become scorched if placed near a radiator or sunny window. Stand on a tray of moist gravel to keep humidity up, or, even better, group with other plants. Keep an ever-watchful eye open for spider mite attack (see pp. 122–3) to which these are prone. Propagation is by rooting side shoots, or by division if these are not readily produced.

room, the one-sided light pulls the new leaves over and prevents them from opening into a rosette. Once the leaves are open, no more growth will occur until the following year and the plant can go back into a room. I once tried putting a plant outside for the summer but the new leaves are so delicate they can be damaged by sun, wind or rain. I have found that plants do better in a John Innes-type compost with a little added peat and grit. If you cannot afford to buy a plant, they can be grown from large seed. The last batch of three seeds I sowed gave rise to two plants. Growth is slow but worth waiting for.

CYCLAMEN ✿

Position: Must have good, direct light during winter. My plants thrive on a south- or west-facing windowsill. As light grows brighter in spring, move back from the window. A cool temperature of 50 to 60°F (10 to 15°C) is optimum. At higher temperatures, especially if combined with poor light, plants wilt and die. The windowsill of an unheated bedroom would be ideal.

Watering: The cyclamen corm sits half-buried at the surface of the compost. There is some danger of it rotting if watering is carried out from above. As a result, we are often advised to water from below by filling the saucer with water. Any water remaining after about an hour should be emptied out. In practice I find that a healthy cyclamen kept in the right conditions will not rot when watered carefully from the top providing the surface of the compost is allowed to feel dry between waterings. A busy person, having watered from below, often forgets to go back and empty the saucer, thus putting the plant in the worse position of being waterlogged.

Feeding: Give liquid feed formulated for flowering house plants every month during winter but fortnightly during spring.

Special points: The florist's cyclamen is derived from a Mediterranean species, C. *persicum*, which is native to Algeria, the Lebanon, and some Greek islands. Cyclamen love a cool, bright position and dislike a

Cyclamen

Left: *Cycas revoluta*

hot, dark place in which they turn yellow and collapse very quickly. Keeping these from year to year is extremely easy and very satisfying. A healthy plant will remain in growth until late spring. When new flower and leaf buds cease to develop, stop water-ing so that leaves turn yellow and die. Rather than take the plant away and store it somewhere out of sight, I prefer to leave it where it is in a light, visible place. My favourite plant remains exposed to the sun much as it would in the Mediterranean regions. Towards late summer, you will notice signs of growth at the top of the corm which is the signal to start watering again. If you had hidden the plant away you might have missed this vital sign of life. I have had the same plant going for three years in the same pot and compost. Perhaps, at the start of its fourth year, I might gently remove the corm just as it starts into growth and repot. A peat-based compost with added sharp sand is ideal.

CYMBIDIUM

Position: Good light with some direct light during winter. A temperature of 55 to 65°F (13 to 18°C) during winter will suit them well. Lower temperatures can be toler-ated but the plant will survive rather than thrive.

Watering: It is difficult to tell when an orchid needs watering because the bark in the compost always looks dry. Try and

Cymbidium

gauge by the weight. Avoid watering too much during winter. But, when the plants are outdoors during summer, give plenty.

Feeding: When plants are growing actively from spring to flowering time, liquid feed every fortnight with a formula for flowering plants at half strength. When watering is reduced during winter, feed monthly or apply as a foliar feed.

Special points: Although cymbidiums are probably amongst the most popular orchids they can be difficult to persuade into flower. By June, when there should be no danger of frost, stand your plant outside in a semi-shady place. Regular watering and feeding coupled with good, even light should ripen up the pseudobulbs and encourage the pro-duction of flower spikes towards the end of summer or autumn. Bring the plant back indoors well before the weather turns cooler. Take great care not to over-water and in dry air stand the pot on a tray of moist pebbles. Repotting should be carried out just after flowering but avoid this until absolutely necessary, as plants flower better when pot-bound. Never use an ordinary potting compost but one specially prepared for orchids. At potting time you can divide the plant up. Leave at least two back bulbs (those with no growth on them) to each bunch of growth.

CYPERUS ☼ Ⓑ ●

Common name: umbrella plant

Position: Good light is preferred but shady corners are tolerated although there will come a point where growth virtually stops due to lack of light. Avoid direct scorching light. Normal temperatures of 60 to 70°F (15 to 21°C) are ideal but 45 to 50°F (7 to 10°C) will be tolerated. Dry air can leave nasty brown edges to tips of leaves.

Watering: These are ideal for people who over-water their plants as this is impossible. Plants will enjoy standing in water constantly.

Feeding: During summer give fortnightly liquid feeds formulated for foliage house plants. During winter one or two feeds will be adequate.

Special points: These are easy house plants to keep. *Cyperus alternifolius* from Malagasy and Mauritius is perhaps the best known but also the most awkward. Long (up to 4-foot/120-cm) stems supporting umbrella-like tufts of leaves have an annoying habit of flopping over. This usually leads to staking which never manages to look elegant. Even *C. alternifolius* 'Gracilis', which is much smaller, has the same problem. I therefore recommend *C. diffusus*, a stocky South African which rarely needs staking. Propagation can be by division but there is a more exciting method. Cut off an umbrella, upturn and plunge head first into a milk bottle of water. Roots, and eventually a young plant, will form from the umbrella and grow upwards. This may seem strange but has nothing to do with the plant's origins on the other side of the world. As they naturally grow near waterways, umbrellas bow down towards the water where roots and new plants grow and eventually float away to make a new colony.

Cyperus diffusus

DAVALLIA ✿

Common name: hare's, deer's, squirrel's or rabbit's foot fern

Position: Good but not direct light is preferred for robust, healthy growth. Lower light results in very thin creeping stems and slow growth. Temperatures between 60 and 65°F (15 to 18°C) suit them but I have seen *D. fijiensis* growing superbly in a frost-free greenhouse.

Watering: Allow the surface of the compost to dry out between waterings. This is of great importance at lower temperatures.

Feeding: Give a balanced liquid feed fortnightly to plants showing active signs of growth. They all have rest periods when less water and no feed will be required.

Special points: With such a strange list of common names you would expect something unusual in the appearance of these plants. Epiphytic ferns more used to scrambling over trees and rocks, they grow long creeping scaly rhizomes (root-like structures) which usually appear furry like animals' feet. They always look as if they are trying to escape from their pots and do very well in hanging baskets. Propagate by division or by cutting away sections of rhizome 2 to 3 inches (5 to 7.5 cm) long. These, pressed into a gritty cutting compost and placed in a polythene bag, will root and send up new fronds. I call my plant a tarantula fern because it looks like a huge spider in a pot with its legs draped over the sides.

Davallia fijiensis

DIEFFENBACHIA ☐

Common name: dumb cane

Position: Good but not direct light is necessary for strong, healthy growth. Also required is a temperature of at least 60°F (15°C) and good humidity, achieved by grouping with other plants or standing on a tray of moist pebbles.

Watering: Allow the surface of the compost time to feel dry between waterings.

Feeding: Give a liquid feed for foliage house plants every fortnight during summer but just monthly during winter when growth slows down.

Special points: First, these plants are not called dumb cane for nothing. Treat them with respect as the sap is poisonous. If you should inadvertently get sap in the mouth it can cause swelling and affect speech. They are extremely handsome foliage plants with leaves of different greens, white and cream depending on variety. After a while they can become leggy and overgrown. Tips of shoots can be used as ordinary cuttings. Stem sec- tions without leaves can also be used. Cut chunks of stem 2 to 3 inches (5 to 7.5 cm) long and nestle them horizontally into some cutting compost. Keep warm and moist (in a polythene bag) until a new shoot grows upwards from a bud on the stem. The remainder of the plant can be cut down to within 1 or 2 inches (2.5 to 5 cm) of the base, cutting above a node or swelling on the stem. In a warm, light position, new shoots will grow from the base.

DIONAEA ☼

Common name: Venus fly trap
Position: Good light absolutely essential. Bright, direct light will not harm the plants. A cool temperature of about 50°F (10°C) is ideal, although lower and higher tempera- tures are tolerated. A windowsill is the best place for them to grow unless you have a cool greenhouse or porch.
Watering: Stand the pot in a tray of shal- low water, kept topped up during summer. In winter, allow a few days between the tray drying up and refilling with water.
Feeding: Not necessary.
Special points: *Dionaea muscipula* comes from the damp soils of coastal regions in North and South Carolina. The amazing ability of the plant to trap insects with its

Dieffenbachia 'Camilla' (left), D. 'Exotica Perfecta' (right)

Dionaea muscipula

leaves and digest them is an adaptation to living in soils where there is very little nour-ishment. The 'trap' is an adapted leaf with nectar-secreting glands which attract insects. The trap closes when the insect touches trigger hairs on the leaf surface. One hair must be touched twice before the trap will close which cuts down on acciden-tal closure – important when it takes the trap twenty-four hours to re-open. It does the health of a plant no good to keep playing with the traps and closing them. Secrets of success include potting new plants into bigger pots when you buy them. Use a com-post consisting of equal parts of peat and sharp sand. Stand the pot in a wide saucer of water to increase humidity. Make sure that flies can get to the plant during its growing period so that it can feed. Never force-feed with mince, dog or cat food.

DIZYGOTHECA

Common name: false aralia
Position: Good but not direct light. To grow tall, large-leaved specimens a tempera-ture of at least 60°F (15°C), preferably more, is required. If this heat is accompanied by dry air then steps must be taken to increase humidity either by grouping with other plants, misting or standing on a tray of moist pebbles. Lower temperatures will be tolerated.
Watering: Allow the surface time to dry out between waterings.

Dizygotheca elegantissima

Feeding: Give fortnightly liquid feeds with a balanced fertiliser during summer, but just once a month during winter and none if growth stops.
Special points: I can remember a *Dizygotheca elegantissima* that I kept for years in a succession of very cold rooms dur-ing the time I was training as a horticulturist at Kew Gardens. Instead of growing lush and tall like its counterparts in tropical greenhouses, it was dwarfed into a compact,

branching shape with smaller leaves and internodes (gaps between leaves). I avoided placing it in draughts, avoided fluctuations in temperature, never overwatered and my plant remained healthy. This is the sort of plant not normally propagated by amateur house plant growers as the method is by seed. However, if you want to try, sow into a pot, place a polythene bag over the top and stand in a warm position out of direct light. Remove the polythene and place on a windowsill as soon as the seedlings show.

DRACAENA ☐ ☼ B

Position: Good but not direct light. In poor light, plants stop growing. In bright, direct light, leaves become scorched. My *Dracaena deremensis* likes the diffused light nine feet away from a west-facing window. Temperatures of between 60 and 70°F (15 to 21°C) are ideal although lower temperatures can be tolerated, particularly by *D. draco*, the Canary Island dragon tree.

1 *Dracaena fragrans*
2 *D. deremensis*
3 *D. marginata*

Watering: Allow the surface of the compost time to dry out between waterings, especially during winter.

Feeding: Fortnightly with liquid feed during the growing season but only a couple of times during winter.

Special points: Those most commonly grown are *D. deremensis, D. marginata*, with its narrow leaves, and *D. fragrans*. All make easy and reliable house plants which respond well to light and regular feeding. My own specimen of the tropical African *D. deremensis* lived for several years in a dark flat and hardly grew at all. For the last few years plenty of light and care have transformed it into a tall, attractive plant. Keep dust off the leaves. When a plant becomes too tall it can be cut down almost to the base in spring from which it will sprout new shoots. The stem can be made into a tip cutting 4 to 6 inches (10 to 15 cm) long. Sections of stem 2 inches (5 cm) long will also root. Cut into 2-inch (5-cm) long sections, each containing at least two nodes (swellings or rings on the stem). These can be pushed vertically or horizontally into the cutting compost and must be kept warm and humid to root (see p. 20).

EUPHORBIA PULCHERRIMA

Common name: poinsettia
Position: Bright but not direct light will keep plants healthy. Warm room temperatures of 60 to 70°F (15 to 21°C) are ideal.

A lower temperature, to 55°F (13°C), can be tolerated but draughts and fluctuations in temperature should be avoided.

Watering: Wait until the surface of the compost has begun to dry out before watering. This is essential as over-watering will result in the general collapse of the plant. Try and use water that has reached room temperature rather than freezing cold straight from the tap.

Feeding: A well-balanced liquid feed no more than once a month will do no harm but is not essential.

Special points: These instructions are for *Euphorbia pulcherrima*, the poinsettia grown for its red-, pink- or cream-coloured bracts. There are other types of euphorbia

Euphorbia pulcherrima

whose cultivation is the same as for succu-lents (see p. 113). The main objective when looking after a poinsettia is to keep the plant healthy and the bracts attractive for as long as possible. I am afraid I then throw my plant away and buy another one the following year. There are, however, those that like the challenge of persuading them into bract again.

As bracts fade, keep the plant on the dry side for about one month. Cut back hard to within 2 to 3 inches (5 to 7.5 cm) of the base and water thoroughly. Given good light and subsequent careful watering, new shoots should grow. These can be taken as 3-inch (7.5-cm) cuttings or left to develop into a new plant. When growth is active, pot on into new compost (a larger-sized pot may not be needed) and, when established in this, feed every fortnight with a high-potash fertiliser. From mid-September onwards it is essential that the plant experiences short days in order to initiate flowers and, of course, bracts. Even a light turned on and off quickly will break the darkness which should be continuous for no less than ten hours per day. The only way to ensure this is to cover and uncover the plant to a rigorous timetable.

X FATSHEDERA ☼ Ⓑ

Common name: tree ivy or fat-headed Lizzie

Position: Needs good but not direct light. Too much light (bright window, unshaded porch or conservatory) results in yellow leaves. A low temperature of 50 to 60°F (10 to 15°C) is preferred although both higher and lower temperatures are tolerated. Dry air at high temperatures can be avoided by standing the plant on a tray of moist gravel.

Watering: Allow the surface of the com-post time to dry out between waterings.

Right: X *Fatshedera lizei*

Feeding: Fortnightly liquid feeds with a formula for foliage house plants during summer. Monthly feeds during winter.

Special points: × *Fatshedera lizei* is a much-grown house plant which resulted as a hybrid between *Fatsia* and *Hedera*. Although tough, I have seen some very sorry specimens of this plant. Ill-health is brought about by over-watering, keeping plain green-leaved kinds too warm and variegated kinds too cold, keeping them in dingy corners or a combination of all three. Well cared for, they make good specimens, especially when three or more are planted together in one pot. One plant tends to look straggly. Tatty plants can be cut back to within 2 to 3 inches (5 to 7.5 cm) of the base during spring, after which several shoots will grow to give a branching habit. Propagation can be by tip cuttings 3 inches (7.5 cm) long. Sections of stem each containing at least two nodes are also successful. Cut above a leaf at the top and below at the bottom, remove the bottom leaf and insert several into a pot of cutting compost.

FATSIA ☼ B

Common name: castor-oil plant
Position: Medium light is preferred. Standing near an east- or north-facing window or some distance into a room with windows facing west or south would be ideal. These plants are supposed to be shade tolerant. However, I subjected one plant to a gloomy corner with depressing results as growth almost stopped. Being hardy enough to grow outside in most districts, this plant can certainly tolerate low temperatures. Normal room temperatures up to 65°F (18°C) cause no problems when combined with good light and humidity.

Watering: Wait until the surface of the compost feels dry to the touch before watering again. Never leave standing in water.

Feeding: Fortnightly during summer but only once or twice during winter.

Special points: The common name given to *Fatsia japonica* is rather misleading as the true castor-oil plant is *Ricinus*. Their leaves do share a similar shape. They are useful foliage plants whose palmate leaves make good patterns against a light background. There is

Fatsia japonica

a variegated-leaved form which would need to be propagated by cuttings or air layering (see p. 21–3). The plain green-leaved *Fatsia japonica* can be germinated from seed.

FICUS ☐ ☼ B

Position: Some direct light during the day is needed for strong growth, particularly for variegated types. As some are tall plants they often stand in corners; this is fine as long as the corner faces a window. I have seen some very good rubber plants standing close to south-facing windows with the harsh light filtered by net curtains. Creeping figs are small trailing plants and good for tumbling over shelves and mantelpieces. Normal room temperatures of 60 to 70°F (15 to 21°C) are ideal, although most figs can tolerate lower temperatures and will grow in a shaded cool conservatory or porch with a minimum temperature of 40°F (5°C).

Watering: Allow the surface of the compost to dry out between waterings, particularly if the plants are growing at lower temperatures. The exception is the creeping fig. This tends to dry out rapidly when well established in its pot and should be kept moist.

Feeding: Fortnightly during summer but only once a month during winter.

Special points: The figs are a handsome group of foliage house plants.

F. elastica is the rubber plant which can

Top: *Ficus elastica* 'Decora'

Ficus pumila 'Sunny'

have dark or coloured leaves according to variety. The biggest problem with these is their tendency to outgrow normal-sized rooms. A rubber plant making a take-over bid has to be tackled. The best solution is to propagate by tip cuttings 4 to 5 inches (10 to 12.5 cm) long or air layering (see p. 21–3). I find it is best not to use hormone rooting powder on these plants as it can damage them. Parent plants can then be replaced by their offspring. The original plant can be pruned hard but tends to send new shoots out sideways which can be a problem. I find it beneficial to mix loam compost with extra peat and grit to create a compost which has more weight than a peat-based mixture. Plants are less likely to topple over when dry.

Ficus benjamina is the popular weeping fig which some people have so many problems with. Large specimens are expensive and cause much heartbreak when they lose leaves. I have watched these plants closely and noticed that whereas during summer they usually grow well, the onset of winter brings problems. Far less light penetrates the house and the side of the plant furthest away from the window begins to lose leaves. This is exacerbated by hot, dry air which can lead to complete defoliation. The answer is to choose a room which is 60 to 65°F (15 to 18°C). Move the plant closer to the window during winter and turn it regularly so

Ficus benjamina (right) and Ficus benjamina 'Starlight'

that all sides receive light. If you suspect dry air of being a problem, stand the pot on a wide tray of moist gravel. A certain amount of leaf-drop is natural and unavoidable. New leaves will grow back in the spring.

Ficus pumila is the creeping fig which will trail or climb, sending out little clinging roots from its stems in humid places. Keep these well watered and they will not prove difficult, rooting easily from 3-inch (7.5-cm) long shoot tip cuttings. Look out for *F. pumila* 'Sunny' which has bold variegated leaves.

FITTONIA

Common name: mosaic or snakeskin plant

Position: Medium light. An ideal temperature would be 65 to 70°F (18 to 21°C). They dislike temperatures lower than 55°F (13°C). The best place for them would be a warm, light, humid place. This makes them excellent for a bathroom shelf, terrarium or bottle garden.

Watering: Keep moist but allow the compost time to dry out slightly between waterings so that it is never waterlogged.

Feeding: Fortnightly during summer but only once or twice during winter.

Special points: There are two different types normally grown. *Fittonia gigantea* has larger leaves with pink veins. When plants are happy they will send up interesting but unshowy spikes of green bracts and small

Fittonia verschaffeltii argyroneura 'Minima'

Gardenia jasminoides

yellowish flowers. The smaller-leaved type has a dreadful name, *Fittonia verschaffeltii argyroneura* 'Minima', and the leaves are veined with creamy white. Both these are grown for their close mounds of foliage. I like to plant several specimens into a wide shallow pot. Small plants are easily raised from shoot tip cuttings.

GARDENIA

Position: Bright but not direct light. They thrive best in temperatures of 50 to 60°F (10 to 15°C) but will grow in temperatures both higher and lower. I have one plant that has tolerated freezing point without dying.

Watering: These are acid-loving plants and should be watered with rainwater. The compost must not dry out as this will cause bud and leaf drop. However, never leave waterlogged and allow the surface of the compost time to dry out between waterings during winter if being kept at low temperatures.

Feeding: When hard tap water has to be used, feed at every watering with a half-strength dilution of a liquid feed for acid-loving plants. If soft rainwater is used, use the same feed at normal strength fortnightly during summer but only once or twice during winter.

Special points: *Gardenia jasminoides* from China is a beautiful plant with shiny leaves and exotic, creamy-coloured perfumed flowers which begin white but mature to butter-yellow. They can infuriate their growers by dropping both leaves and flower buds at the slightest provocation. Never allow them to dry out, avoid moving the plants when in bud, remember they are lime-haters which means they need a compost for acid-loving plants and you should succeed with them. After a while plants may become leggy and in need of pruning. This is best carried out in spring, cutting back some of the older stems hard to promote new growth.

GERBERA

Common name: Barberton daisy
Position: Bright, direct light. Temperatures of 55 to 60°F (13 to 15°C) are ideal. Higher temperatures would be a problem but these plants can withstand temperatures just high enough to keep frost out provided they are kept on the dry side. Good plants for a windowsill or porch.

Gerbera

Watering: Allow the surface of the compost to dry out before watering again as these are prone to problems caused by over-watering.
Feeding: Use a liquid feed for flowering plants fortnightly during summer and once or twice during winter unless growth has completely slowed down.
Special points: These are well worth growing for their vivid, daisy-like flowers on long stems. They can be propagated by seed or by dividing the clump that the plant makes. The biggest problem likely to be encountered is with watering. In cold weather I would water from below to avoid the possibility of rotting the crown at compost level.

GUZMANIA

Position: Good but not direct light. Keep them close to a window or they will not come into flower again. Temperatures of 65 to 70°F (18 to 21°C) are ideal but lower temperatures down to 50°F (10°C) are tolerated.
Watering: These plants grow epiphytically up in the branches of trees in the wild. They would have a very limited root system and catch water in their rosettes which form small 'urns' like those of the urn plant (*Aechmea fasciata*) to which they are related. As a result they dislike being too wet at the roots. Allow the surface of the compost time to dry out between waterings.

71

Guzmania 'Grand Prix' (left back), G. 'Amaranth' (right back), G. 'Minor Red' (front)

The rosettes do not hold much but are worth filling up when watering.

Feeding: Give a liquid feed every fortnight during the summer but only once or twice during winter.

Special points: These are exotic-looking plants which will stay in flower for a long period after settling down in your home. When the flower spike eventually fades, cut it off leaving the remains of the flowered rosette which will gradually die off (this might take as long as a year). Offsets will appear around this old rosette which seem unwilling to form their own roots if taken off the plant. Leave the whole clump to grow on, feeding and watering well, until the new rosettes reach flowering size. Once the old rosette has died away, the clump can be divided or repotted. Use an open compost

made by adding extra sharp sand and coarse peat to a peat-based compost. There are now many *Guzmania* hybrids including the Scarlet Star, G. 'Minor Red', and tall Flaming Torch types like G. 'Amaranth' and G. 'Claret'.

GYNURA □ ☼ B

Common name: velvet plant
Position: Likes plenty of light to keep the leaves healthy and well coloured. I keep mine on an east-facing windowsill. North-facing would be acceptable but south- or west-facing might be too bright and lead to scorching. Temperatures of 60 to 65°F (15 to 18°C) are ideal but can go down to 55°F (13°C) without doing any harm.
Watering: Allow the surface of the com-

Gynura sarmentosa

post time to dry out before watering again.

Feeding: Liquid feed with a balanced formula every fortnight during summer but just once or twice during winter. Avoid giving a high-nitrogen feed for foliage plants as this is likely to spoil the compact, colourful habit of the leaves, making them too green and sappy.

Special points: *Gynura sarmentosa* is the species most grown for its incredibly soft, furry, bright purple leaves. Plants begin to trail and climb as they grow older. If you want to keep them bushy, pinch out the growing tips regularly. This will also prevent the formation of flowers which look like those of groundsel and smell awful. A succession of young plants can be ensured by taking shoot tip cuttings which root easily. Keep these cuttings in a light place but shaded from full sun and do not over-water.

HEDERA ☼ B

Common name: ivy

Position: Although plants can tolerate low light and conjure up pictures of native *Hedera helix* (English ivy) growing under trees, they do not thrive unless given good light. Make sure they have good but not direct light and they will grow fast and happily. Whereas a temperature of 50 to 55°F (10 to 13°C) is ideal, they can tolerate higher temperatures although steps should be taken to increase humidity by standing with other plants or placing the pot on a tray

of moist pebbles. Lower temperatures are easily tolerated.

Watering: Allow the surface of the compost time to dry out between waterings.

Feeding: During summer, feed fortnightly but reduce this to just a couple of times during winter.

Special points: Ivies come in all sorts of shapes and sizes of leaf. Most are varieties of

Hedera canariensis 'Gloire de Marengo' (back), Hedera helix 'Goldchild' (front right), Hedera helix 'Kolibri' (front left)

H. helix. The mottled silver leaves of 'Glacier' and gold of 'Lutzii' are old favourites as is the arrow-headed foliage of 'Sagittifolia'. There is also *H. canariensis,* the Canary Island ivy, and its variegated form, *H. c.* 'Gloire de Marengo', which has large leaves of grey-green and creamy white. The variegated Persian ivy, *H. colchica* 'Dentata Variegata', is another favourite. A carefully chosen mixture of different ivies arranged in a basket planter can look very attractive and are certainly easy to grow. Provide canes or a moss pole for support and be ever on the look-out for spider mite (see pp. 122–3) to which these are prone. Shoot-tip cuttings root easily in spring, even doing so in water.

HIBISCUS

Position: Good light, close to a window with a few hours of direct light each day. Normal room temperatures of 60 to 70°F (15 to 21°C) are ideal although fluctuations are to be avoided. However, if kept on the dry side during winter they can withstand minimum temperatures almost down to freezing point. Plants will grow again in spring from dormant buds on the stem. This makes them suitable for cool porches or lean-tos.

Watering: When growing in a warm house, allow the top surface of the compost to just begin to dry out between waterings. If you expect them to survive low temperatures then they should be kept much drier,

two-thirds of the compost drying out between waterings. The leaves usually fall off under these conditions so do not worry.

Feeding: When actively growing, feed fortnightly with a well-balanced feed for flowering plants. Do not feed if the plants are dormant.

Special points: *Hibiscus rosa-sinensis* varieties include a range of colours and have large, wonderfully exotic flowers. Newly bought plants have the annoying habit of dropping their flower buds, usually due to the shock of being moved, and to fluctuating temperatures. Avoid over-watering. As described above, they can either be kept

Hibiscus rosa-sinensis cultivar

green and growing all year round in a warm room or can withstand much lower temperatures if necessary in a dormant state. Either way, older plants will become leggy and should be pruned in spring to encourage fresh stems. Always cut just above a node. Shoot-tip cuttings 3 to 4 inches (7.5 to 10 cm) long root easily during spring and summer.

HIPPEASTRUM

Common name: amaryllis
Position: Good light is essential if you do not want your plant to become leggy and collapse. Temperatures of between 55 and 65°F (13 to 18°C) are ideal. Lower temperatures can be tolerated.
Watering: When actively growing, keep the compost moist but not waterlogged. Do not water during the resting period.
Feeding: When the leaves are growing strongly, feed every fortnight with a high-potash fertiliser to encourage flower bud production for next year. Obviously no feeding is needed during the resting phase.
Special points: Hippeastrum or 'amaryllis' bulbs make excellent gifts and are usually started into growth during winter. The bulb should be planted into a pot about an inch (2.5 cm) larger all the way around the bulb. Leave the top third of the bulb above soil. If the roots feel very dry and shrivelled, it is a good plan to soak the base in water for a couple of hours before planting. You would

be very unlucky if your plant did not flower as the bud should already be formed inside the bulb when you buy it. After flowering, take good care of the plant so that it can prepare itself for next year's flowering. Unfortunately they rarely show signs of dying down on their own so, during summer, stop watering and make the plant die down. Rest for a period of three months, then begin watering again, after which the new flower bud should appear. Although this is the accepted way of growing these plants I do know people who allow their plants to stay in growth all year round with great success. Given good light, water and

Hippeastrum

food, they retain their leaves and sometimes flower twice a year.

HOWEA ☐ ☼ Ⓑ ●

Common name: kentia palm
Position: Good but not direct light, especially during summer when leaves might be scorched. I keep my 7-foot (2-metre) tall specimen (which has made regular appearances on *Gardeners' World*) about 8 feet (2.4 metres) away from an east-facing window with great success. The temperature they prefer is 60 to 65°F (15 to 18°C). They can tolerate lower temperatures of 50°F (10°C) but at higher temperatures begin to show signs of stress caused by dry air; usually brown, dry tips to the leaves.
Watering: The surface of the compost should just begin to feel dry before watering again. Make sure water has penetrated to the bottom of the pot if the plant is in a large container. I am sure many large specimens are killed because they are given too little water at a time. Slightly less water is required during winter.
Feeding: Fortnightly with a balanced liquid feed in summer, monthly during winter.
Special points: *Howea belmoreana* is most commonly grown and used to be called *Kentia*. They are great dust-collectors and should be dusted regularly with a soft cloth.

Left: Howea belmoreana

Dirty leaves can be wiped with a damp cloth only when the dust has been removed. Keep a vigilant watch for spider mite which can be a problem (see pp. 122–3).

HOYA

Common name: wax plant, honey plant
Position: For plants to flower they must have some direct light every day, so grow close to a window. Temperatures of between 60 and 70°F (15 to 21°C) are ideal but with careful watering *Hoya carnosa* can tolerate temperatures as low as 45 to 50°F (7 to 10°C). A windowsill during winter can be too cold at night, causing leaves to turn yellow and drop off.
Watering: These plants have shallow, rather delicate roots used to receiving a lot of air and as a result must be watered carefully to avoid suffocation. Allow the surface of the compost time to dry out between waterings, especially if plants are being asked to grow in lower temperatures than they might prefer. Try to use water at room temperature.
Feeding: Over-feeding can cause too much leafy growth at the expense of flowers. Feed every three weeks during active growing periods only, with a high-potash fertiliser to encourage flowers.
Special points: A beautiful group of plants, there are several different types to choose from. One of the best known is *Hoya carnosa* and its varieties with variegated or

Hoya bella

coloured leaves. These are strong climbers, which when fairly pot-bound, given plenty of light and not over-fed, will produce clusters of unusual creamy star-shaped flowers with pink centres during summer. These are fragrant, especially at night, and exude sticky nectar. *Hoya bella* is a trailing type with narrower leaves and daintier, beautifully formed flowers. This is extremely prone to over-watering but must not be allowed to dry right out, and needs more warmth than *H. carnosa*. Sometimes offered for sale is *Hoya multiflora*, really more of a tall shrub than a twining climber. Flowers

are smaller and yellower than the other two and it also needs warmth to do well. With all hoyas it is important not to cut off seemingly dead flower heads. The stalk will remain on the plant and produce further flower buds. Shoot-tip cuttings 3 to 4 inches (7.5 to 10 cm) long will root easily given warm, humid conditions out of harsh sunlight (see p. 16). The national collection of hoyas is kept by the Welsh Mountain Zoo, Colwyn Bay.

HYDRANGEA

Position: Bright light is required to keep growth healthy and sturdy. However, light from a south- or west-facing window might be too bright. I usually group mine near an east-facing window and they stay in flower

Hydrangea

for long periods if kept below 60°F (15°C). Coolness and light are essential.

Watering: These plants dry out very quickly and need watering at least twice as often as ordinary house plants. If they wilt badly, leave them standing in water for a few hours until thoroughly moist and do not let it happen again.

Feeding: These plants are only indoors for a couple of months but should be liquid fed every two to three weeks with a well-balanced formula. Blue-flowered kinds will benefit from a formula for acid-loving plants.

Special points: These are usually bought in bud, if looked after well will remain in flower for a couple of months, and should then be planted outside when all danger of frost is past (they are hardy but will have produced unnaturally soft growth in the house). Do not forget that they like a moist, shady spot and that pink varieties turn blue if planted in an acid soil while blue varieties turn pink if planted in an alkaline soil.

Hypoestes phyllostachya

HYPOESTES

Common name: polka-dot plant

Position: Good light is necessary for strong, sturdy plants and brightly coloured leaves. However, full sun during summer might scorch. Temperatures of 60 to 70°F (15 to 21°C) are ideal but can drop to 55°F (13°C) without harming plants. These little plants do well in a terrarium provided it is placed in good light and the growing tips are pinched out regularly.

Watering: Allow the surface of the compost time to dry out between waterings.

Feeding: Fortnightly during summer with a well-balanced liquid feed. Only two or three feeds will be necessary during winter.

Special points: *Hypoestes phyllostachya (sanguinolenta)* are small, attractive plants grown for their rather silly pink or white spotted leaves. Even in good light, they will become tall and straggly if growing tips are not pinched out to make bushy plants. After a while, tiny purplish flowers will appear. Shortly after this the plants begin to look sad but at the base a set of furry new shoots will form. Cut back all the old growth and let the new take over. Cuttings 3 inches (7.5 cm) long root easily, even in water. New plants can also be raised from seed.

IMPATIENS ✳ ☐ Ⓑ

Common name: busy Lizzy
Position: Good but not direct light. Normal room temperatures of 60 to 70°F (15 to 21°C) are ideal. Lower temperatures down to 55°F (13°C) are tolerated but higher temperatures are usually accompanied by dry air which they dislike.
Watering: Allow the surface to dry out between waterings. They enjoy being moist but not waterlogged.
Feeding: While producing active growth, feed fortnightly during summer but just a couple of times in winter with a well-balanced liquid feed.
Special points: I can remember, not so long ago, when the only busy Lizzy widely grown was the rather lanky, pale-pink-flowered *Impatiens walleriana* originally from Tanzania and Mozambique. Now there are all sorts of wonderful hybrids. Some are grown mainly as shade-tolerant bedding plants. Before the frosts these can be lifted, potted, cut back and enjoyed as house plants which will flower all winter in good light. There are white, pinks, reds, oranges, doubles and rosebuds to choose from. When they become straggly, cut hard back to promote new growth. Cuttings root easily in water. A very choice group are the New Guinea Hybrids which have larger, more exotic-looking flowers and attractive leaves of red, or with bright variegations. They need good humidity and are prone to spider mite at high temperatures.

Impatiens New Guinea Hybrids

JASMINUM

Common name: jasmine
Position: Good light is essential for flower production, so place near a window. These plants are really at their best in a cool porch or conservatory. However, they will grow adequately in temperatures up to 60 to 65°F (15 to 18°C). Their favourite winter temperature is probably about 50°F (10°C) but this can go down almost to freezing.
Watering: Keep moist without standing in water when growth is at its most active (spring and summer). Otherwise just allow the surface of the compost to dry out in between.

Jasminum polyanthum

Feeding: Fortnightly during summer with a well-balanced liquid feed.

Special points: *Jasminum polyanthum* or Chinese jasmine is usually sold early in the year, having been forced into flower. There are frequently problems with the beautiful white fragrant flowers which turn yellow in bud and fall off in horror at the trauma of being moved. The key to success is to give good light and an even temperature. These plants can grow enormous and will need a climbing frame. You can keep them in a circle but this involves training and pruning side shoots back to within one or two buds of older stems after flowering. Four-inch (10-cm) long summer cuttings root easily.

KALANCHOE　✻ ☐ Ⓑ

Common names: *Kalanchoe blossfeldiana* is often called flaming Katy, while *K. daigremontianum* is the Mexican hat plant or devil's backbone.

Position: Good, bright light is necessary for sturdy growth and flowering. Suitable for a sunny windowsill. Normal room temperatures of 60 to 65°F (15 to 18°C) are acceptable but a winter rest at lower temperatures of 45 to 50°F (7 to 10°C) for *K. daigremontianum*, and others grown primarily for their leaves, is preferred. Most can tolerate temperatures dropping to 40°F (5°C), making them ideal for a porch or lean-to. *K. blossfeldiana cultivars* are the most commonly grown and the best adapted to average living-room temperatures.

Kalanchoe blossfeldiana cultivars

Kalanchoe 'Wendy'

fade, when, realistically, they should be thrown out. They can be trimmed back and will flower again, though less profusely. *K.* 'Tessa' and similar cultivars are the dainty hanging basket types, whose stems of succulent leaves trail and produce pale-orange, bell-shaped flowers. They will become straggly with age but can be cut back, after flowers have faded, to the top of the basket from where they will sprout again. *K.* 'Wendy' is more upright, with larger cream-tipped rose-pink flowers. *K. daigremontianum* is upright with almost diamond-shaped, succulent leaves which bear small plantlets along the edges. These, rooted, will make new plants. Similar in style is *K. tubiflora*, which has tube-like leaves bearing a cluster of plantlets at the ends.

Watering: Allow the surface of the compost time to dry out between waterings. In winter, water most types except *K. blossfeldiana* very sparingly. *K. blossfeldiana* is in flower during winter and thus requires more warmth and water.

Feeding: Give a well-balanced liquid feed monthly during summer but not at all during winter for those being grown for their leaves. *K. blossfeldiana cultivars*, *K.* 'Tessa', *K.* 'Wendy' and others flowering during winter should be fed monthly during this time.

Special points: *Kalanchoe blossfeldiana cultivars* with flowers of red, pink, orange or yellow are very popular house plants which should last for several weeks before flowers

Kalanchoe 'Tessa'

LEEA

Position: Good but not direct light is essential for sturdy growth. Normal room temperatures of 60 to 70°F (15 to 21°C) are ideal but should not drop below this for any length of time. Avoid fluctuations.

Watering: Allow the surface of the compost time to feel dry between waterings. Use water at room temperature and never leave any in the saucer.

Feeding: Fortnightly during spring, summer and autumn with a well-balanced liquid feed. Only once or twice during winter.

Special points: *Leea coccinea* is rarely seen for sale except as seed. It is *Leea* 'Burgundy' that appears in garden centres. Aptly named, it is grown for its delicate, deep burgundy-coloured foliage. These plants

Leea 'Burgundy'

seem to keel over and start dying at the first hint of trouble which can be a sudden drop in temperature, or if left standing in cold water for any length of time. My own plant, which had grown healthily at 60°F (15°C) in an east-facing room about 10 feet (3 metres) from the window for several months, nearly died after an over-enthusiastic watering before going away one Christmas. After ideal conditions were restored it took four months for it to recover and begin growing again.

LITHOPS ☐ ☼ B

Common name: living stones, stone, pebble or mimicry plants

Position: Must have the best, bright light available. A south- or west-facing window is ideal. A temperature of 50 to 65°F (10 to 18°C) is best, though lower temperatures, almost down to freezing, can be tolerated. My own plants thrive on the west-facing windowsill of an unheated bedroom.

Watering: Between October and March they should have no water at all, even if they begin to look a little shrivelled. The first spring watering is wonderful because they really swell up and look happy. Spring brings the light they need to grow after this dormant phase. The old pair of leaves will separate and a new pair push their way through. During spring and summer, water when the surface becomes dry, much as you would for any plant.

Lithops

Feeding: Use a half-strength liquid feed formulated for cacti and succulents about once a month during the growing season only.

Special points: A fascinating group of succulents, lithops look just like the stones that would surround them in their native African deserts. They will produce large, usually white or yellow, daisy-like flowers which look incongruous on such diminutive plants. Plants are easily raised from seed which can be sown during summer. Do not disturb or prick out the small plants until the following spring when they can be spaced out in a pan of well-drained cactus compost (see p. 40). Finish the surface off with gravel and stones. Some kinds form clumps which can be divided up in summer when they become too large.

Right: *Maranta leuconeura kerchoviana* (right), *M. leuconeura erythroneura* (left)

MARANTA □ B ●

Common name: prayer plant, rabbit's foot

Position: Good but not direct light. Bright light can scorch and bleach the foliage. Normal room temperatures of 60 to 70°F (15 to 21°C) are ideal. They do not grow well under 50°F (10°C). Avoid positions of dry heat, raising humidity by standing on trays of moist pebbles if necessary.

Watering: During the growing season keep the compost moist but not saturated. During winter allow the surface of the compost time to dry out between waterings.

Feeding: Fortnightly with a formula for foliage plants when growing actively. Only feed a couple of times during winter.

Special points: These tropical Americans are referred to as prayer plants because they

share the habit of folding together and rais-ing their leaves at night, presumably to pre-vent moisture loss from the surface of the leaf, when it is not required to absorb light for plant food-making processes. *Maranta leuconeura erythroneura* is often called the herringbone plant, on account of the pattern of red veins on the leaf. *M. leuconeura kerchoviana* is called rabbit's foot because the dark green blotches between the veins do, with some imagination, look like the tracks of a rabbit's paws. Low-growing foli-age plants, they are suitable for large terraria and bottle gardens and make nice additions to planted bowls. They can be propagated by division in the spring or by taking 3- to 4-inch (7.5- to 10-cm) cuttings which will root in water or cutting compost.

MONSTERA □ ☼ B ●

Common name: Swiss cheese plant
Position: Although probably one of the most tolerant of house plants, they will grow much better in good, though not direct, light. A temperature of between 60 and 70°F (15 to 21°C) is ideal. At higher tem-peratures dry air might be a problem. Lower temperatures down to 45°F (7°C) can be tolerated but are certainly not appreciated.
Watering: Allow the surface of the com-post time to dry out slightly between waterings.
Feeding: Liquid feed fortnightly during spring, summer and autumn but only once

or twice during winter.
Special points: A happy 'cheese plant' will romp away and cause problems by growing too large. Long aerial roots form along the stems but fortunately no harm is caused to the plant if these are cut off. It has been said that these should be poked back into the pot but there is a limit to how many the pot will accommodate. In the wild, as the plant climbs up tall trees, these aerial roots provide anchorage and absorb water

Monstera deliciosa

and nutrients closer to the growing shoots. In your living-room they are not likely to find a nice pocket of compost behind the television. They will attach themselves to a moist moss pole, used instead of a stake to support the plant, but it is not easy to keep these moist in the house. Monsteras can be pruned hard in spring, cutting above a leaf close to the base. Given a light position, a new stem or stems will form and take over. To propagate, take large shoot-tip cuttings or portions of stem each containing two nodes, cutting above the top leaf and below the bottom which is then removed. They also respond well to air layering (see pp. 21–3). Young plants sometimes take a while to develop the familiar holes in the leaf that give them their common name. Rather insignificant, though large and interesting flowers, typical of the *Araceae* (arum) family, are sometimes formed and can be followed by edible fruits.

MUSA

Common name: banana plant
Position: Good light is essential with at least three to four hours of direct sunlight each day. I used to think it would be difficult to grow good specimens in the house. However, I was proved wrong by some friends who grew a massive 7-foot (2-metre) tall specimen in a large, north-facing bay window. Unfortunately it did not flower and set fruit until donated to other friends with a

conservatory. Fruit formation usually depends on much higher humidity levels than can be provided in the home. A south-facing window might be too bright during summer and scorch the leaves. Normal room temperatures of 60 to 70°F (15 to 21°C) are ideal for most types though dry air might be a problem, helped by standing the pot on a tray of moist pebbles. Cool temperatures of 40 to 50°F (5 to 10°C) are preferred by *Musa basjoo*, the Japanese banana, which can withstand virtually freezing conditions. This, however, only produces small fruit.
Watering: Allow the surface of the compost time to dry out between waterings.

Musa X paradisiaca 'Dwarf Cavendish'

Less water will be required in winter, but keep more moist during summer.

Feeding: Give fortnightly liquid feeds while plants are actively growing. No feeding during winter.

Special points: The best type to go for is probably *Musa* × *paradisiaca* 'Dwarf Cavendish' which will not grow too tall (5 feet/ 150 cm) and is the one most likely to flower and fruit in a pot. Should a plant fruit, that portion of the plant will gradually die off. An offset should appear at the base which will take over from the fruited plant. When the old plant begins to look sorry for itself, remove the new plant and pot this up separately. This could take a long time to flower and fruit. Plants can be raised from seed.

NEOREGELIA □

Common name: blushing bromeliad

Position: Good but not too much direct light is essential for maintaining healthy growth and vivid leaf-colour. An east- or north-facing window is ideal. A temperature between 60 and 70°F (15 to 21°C) suits them well. They are not worth trying to grow below 50°F (10°C), while high temperatures bring problems of dry air. Raise humidity by standing the pot on a tray of moist pebbles and by misting regularly.

Watering: As these plants are naturally epiphytic, growing up in the branches of trees rather than on the ground, their root systems are not very strong and are suscep-

Neoregelia carolinae 'Tricolor'

tible to over-watering. Allow the surface of the compost time to dry out and admit air between waterings. The 'urn'-like rosettes can be filled with water.

Feeding: Fortnightly during summer and monthly during winter with a well-balanced liquid feed.

Special points: *Neoregelia carolinae* 'Tricolor' is the type most commonly grown. The centre of the variegated leaves is a vivid pink, making this an astonishingly attractive, though hardly subtle foliage plant. Small blue flowers appear in the 'urn', often under the water it holds. Offsets, produced around the base of the parent plant, can be removed and potted up separately. If these have no roots of their own, insert into a pot of cutting compost and place a polythene bag over the top to keep warm and moist until rooted. A good potting compost is peat-based with added sharp sand and coarse peat.

NEPHROLEPIS ●

Common name: Boston or ladder fern
Position: Good light but out of direct sun. My plants grow well at the far side of a room opposite the window. Temperatures between 60 and 70°F (15 to 21°C) are ideal. They do not grow well below 50°F (10°C) although they can tolerate temperatures down to 40°F (5°C). At high temperatures, dry air causes fronds to turn brown and dry. Increase humidity by misting or standing the pot on a tray of moist gravel.
Watering: These ferns must never be allowed to dry out or they will turn brown and start dropping pinnae (leaflets). Many are grown in hanging baskets when they are even more prone to drying out.
Feeding: Fortnightly during active growth but just monthly during winter.

Nephrolepis

Special points: *Nephrolepis exaltata* and its varieties are the most commonly grown and are a beautiful group of ferns. They often come to grief because they are exposed to too hot and dry a room, or their owners forget to water them often enough. One plant often turns out to be a colony. Runners are produced from the original plant's rhizome, which root themselves into the compost around the parent. These can be taken separately and grown on, or the colony taken out of its pot and divided. Like other ferns, they can be propagated by spores (see p. 14).

NOLINA ☐ ☼ Ⓑ

Common name: pony-tail palm, elephant's foot, bottle palm
Position: Good light is essential to prevent the plant from becoming weak and spindly. Three to four feet (about a metre) away from a south-facing window proves ideal for my plant as does a temperature of 60°F (15°C). Mexican in origin, higher temperatures are no problem if accompanied by good light, otherwise plants can become drawn. Temperatures of 40°F (5°C) can be tolerated if the plants are kept dry during winter. My plant thrives in an unheated bedroom.
Watering: Well able to store moisture in its swollen stem, *Nolina* is best treated as a succulent. Water normally in summer, allowing the surface of the compost time to

Nolina recurvata

dry out between waterings. During winter allow the compost to become dry between waterings.

Feeding: Every month with a liquid feed for cacti and succulents during spring, summer and autumn. No feed during winter.

Special points: The common names are easy to understand when you see *Nolina recurvata* (previously called *Beaucarnea*). The swollen base leads up to a stem crowned with a wild tuft of narrow, stiff leaves that can give a nasty cut if handled wrongly. They make large, interesting specimen plants which in the right position are very easy to grow. The tips of leaves tend to dry up and turn brown with age which is irritating but rather unavoidable. They are

supposed to like a loam-based compost but mine has been happy in a peat-based compost with added sharp sand.

PELARGONIUM ✳ ☐ ☼ Ⓑ

Position: Good, direct light is essential, making these excellent windowsill plants. Normal room temperatures are a little high for the plants during winter when they prefer a cool 50°F (10°C) and can tolerate down to about 38°F (3°C).

Watering: When plants are growing fast, usually during spring and summer, water freely though allowing the surface of the compost time to dry out between waterings. During winter far less water is needed.

Feeding: Give a high-potash liquid feed during periods of active growth, usually spring, summer and autumn.

Special points: Pelargoniums, though associated more with greenhouse and garden, do make colourful, summery windowsill plants. They have acquired the common name of geranium but I do not encourage this as there is a genus of hardy plants to which this name rightfully belongs. The commonest types are the zonal pelargoniums, often sold as bedding plants, which can be potted up and make very economical house plants. For the connoisseur, named varieties propagated by cuttings rather than seed can be bought from specialist growers. A perusal of a specialist list will soon enlighten the novice as to the range of

1 *Pelargonium* 'Mabel Grey'
2 *P. crispum* 'Variegatum'
3 *P.* 'Appleblossom Rosebud'
4 Miniature *Pelargonium* 'Goblin'

different pelargoniums available. Ivy-leaved, used for hanging baskets, make wonderful trailing plants. Regals come into flower dur- and early summer and are a little more ten- der than zonal pelargoniums. Then there is a range of hybrids and species with different flowers and some with scented leaves. Some species bear little obvious resemblance to bedding pelargoniums but are fascinating to grow. If they look like succulent plants then treat them as such. Among my favourites are the dainty *P.* × *fragrans* 'Variegatum' with compact bushy form and delicate pale-pink flowers, *P.* 'Mabel Grey', an upright plant with leaves that smell the strongest of any lemon-scented plant I can think of, *P. violaceum* for its silvery leaves and bright pink and white flowers, and *P. echinatum album*. Do not over-water these plants, most of which have their origins in South Africa. Prune most of the shrubby types hard in spring to keep growth compact and keep an eye open for a disease called rust (see p. 125) which sometimes strikes. Most kinds can be propagated by 3-inch (7.5-cm) long shoot-tip cuttings. Never enclose these in a polythene bag as they tend to rot.

PELLAEA ☼

Common name: button fern
Position: Bright light will damage the fronds but growth will stop in a gloomy cor- ner, so these ferns need medium light. Tem- peratures of 50 to 60°F (10 to 15°C) are ideal. Lower temperatures can be tolerated but higher temperatures usually result in dry air which is lethal. These are good ferns for a large terrarium.
Watering: Never allow the compost to dry out but do not leave standing in water.
Feeding: Fortnightly with a well-balanced liquid feed during spring, summer and autumn but once a month during winter.

Pellaea falcata (right), Pellaea rotundifolia (left)

Special points: *Pellaea rotundifolia* looks and sounds easy to grow, but in my experience this fern from Australia, New Zealand and the Norfolk Islands is not. They will not tolerate any drying out at the roots or dry air. Fluctuations of temperature result in leaves turning yellow and dropping off. However, when they are healthy they make handsome foliage plants which look good planted up into a basket. Clumps can be divided by cutting the rhizome so that the divisions each have rhizome and fronds. Spores can be sown (see p. 14).

PEPEROMIA

Common name: pepper elder
Position: Good light, with some direct sunlight, is necessary for sturdy growth. Normal room temperatures of 60 to 70°F (15 to 21°C) are ideal as they languish at temperatures below 50°F (10°C).

Watering: As many of these are naturally epiphytic, scrambling over tree trunks and rocks in the tropics, they are not used to growing in deep soil and do not have very well-developed root systems. As such, they need very careful watering, allowing the compost to begin to dry out sufficiently to let air into the soil before watering again.

Feeding: A well-balanced liquid feed should be given every three weeks during summer but only once or twice during the winter.

Special points: I have always been very fond of the peperomias and once grew a large collection of them. Provided they have good light, warm temperatures and are not over-watered, they are easy to grow. *P. caperata* must be one of the most common

Peperomia caperata 'Red Lunar' (left), P. caperata (centre), P. magnoliaefolia (right)

with its small, dark green, crinkly leaves. This can be propagated by leaf cuttings. Cut off a healthy leaf, with stalk, and insert this into cutting compost so that the point where the leaf joins the stalk is in contact with the compost. The variegated form will not come true from leaf cuttings and must be propagated by short shoot-tip cuttings. *P. argyreia*, the water-melon peperomia, can also be propagated from leaf cuttings. In this case a cut can be made across the leaf which is then inserted vertically with the cut ends of the leaf veins in touch with the soil. *P. magnoliaefolia* has rounded variegated leaves and is propagated by more conventional shoot-tip cuttings. Although *P. caperata* and others have quite attractive flowers, the only one to feature greatly in this department is *P. resediflora* whose white flowers on red stalks are most attractive.

Phalaenopsis

PHALAENOPSIS

Common name: moth orchid
Position: Good light, with perhaps a few hours of direct light. The bright light from a south- or west-facing window might scorch the leaves. Good light is so important for flowering that it might pay to move plants closer to windows, though not draughty ones, during winter. Temperatures of 65 to 70°F (18 to 21°C) are ideal, coupled with high humidity best provided by standing the plant on a tray of moist pebbles. Lower temperatures can be tolerated but plants are not

so likely to grow well and flower.
Watering: As these orchids should be grown in a special orchid compost composed of bark, it is best to feel the weight of the pot before watering again as the surface of a bark compost usually looks dry.
Feeding: Give a liquid feed that is also a foliar feed every fortnight at half strength.
Special points: These are one of the orchids most likely to flower well in the home. They would naturally grow in tropical forests, clinging to the bark of trees with

their fleshy epiphytic roots. Use an orchid compost when potting. They often send roots up over the compost and edge of the pot as though trying to escape. There are many different hybrids to choose from, all with exquisite, long-lasting flowers. Do not cut off the stalks that have just flowered as these can sprout out new stems with more buds. Instead, as the flower buds fade, cut back to a place on the flower stem between two nodes (swellings on the stem). Eventually new plants will form around the base of older ones. When they appear to have grown a few roots of their own, these can carefully be separated and potted up. I prefer to leave plants to grow into good clumps. Growing the orchids to flowering size is much easier in a greenhouse so investing in a good-sized plant will guarantee better flowering potential in the house.

PHILODENDRON ☐ ☼ Ⓑ ●

Position: As most of these climb up trees in the tropics, clinging with epiphytic roots or sending out aerial roots as they grow, they can be assumed to tolerate some shade, making them excellent house plants. Some good light, however, does ensure healthy, rapid growth. A temperature between 60 and 70°F (15 and 21°C) is ideal and, although lower temperatures are tolerated, they are not worth growing much under 50°F (10°C).

Watering: Allow the surface of the com-

post to feel slightly dry to the touch before watering again.

Feeding: Fortnightly with a well-balanced liquid feed during summer, but only every month during winter.

Special points: *Philodendron scandens* is the climbing or trailing sweetheart plant with heart-shaped leaves. One of the smaller of the group, it is very accommodating. Straggly specimens can be cut back hard just above leaf joints from where new shoots will

Philodendron scandens

grow. Shoot-tip cuttings root very easily. *Philodendron* 'Burgundy' is a hefty climber with red leaves and *P. bipinnatifidum* is a wide-spreading plant needing a lot of space for its large leaves. All climbing types prefer a moss-pole for support. Large shoot-tip cuttings can be taken, or fresh plants grown from seed.

PILEA

Position: Good but not direct light. Normal room temperatures of 60 to 70°F (15 to 21°C). They do not grow very well under 50°F (10°C) excpt *P. microphylla* which can go down to 40°F (5°C).

Watering: Allow the surface of the compost to become dry between waterings. Never leave water in the saucer.

Feeding: A well-balanced liquid feed fortnightly during summer but just monthly during winter.

Special points: I am very fond of these small, compact foliage plants. Although not making much of a specimen on its own, a pilea can be grouped with others to make a very attractive bowl. There is *Pilea cadierei*, its deep green leaves marked with silver blotches, known as the aluminium or friendship plant. *P. mollis* 'Moon Valley' has crinkled lime-green and brown leaves, *P.* 'Silver Tree' narrow silver-striped leaves, *P. spruciana* 'Norfolk' has a very metallic silver

Left: *Philodendron* hybrid

Pilea cadierei

and bronze look, while *P. microphylla* is the artillery plant with lots of tiny bright-green leaves. Plants root easily from 3-inch (7.5-cm) shoot-tip cuttings. A good idea with the lower-growing kinds is to plant three or more rooted cuttings into a shallow pot for a quick effect.

PLATYCERIUM

Common name: stag's horn or elk's horn fern

Position: Bright light is needed for healthy growth but summer sunlight close to a south-facing window might scorch the fronds. I keep my plant 6 feet (1.8 metres)

Platycerium

away from an east-facing window. They look very tropical but in my experience most will tolerate temperatures as low as 45°F (7°C) without serious problems. A temperature of 60 to 70°F (15 to 21°C) is probably optimum for most, with higher temperatures tolerated if humidity can also be maintained.

Watering: This is not easy as these plants are naturally epiphytic and would grow high up in the branches of trees. The humid atmosphere around them would prevent their rather reduced root systems from drying up. When grown in a pot, the large infertile fronds make watering from the top difficult if not impossible. I stand my plant in a bucket of water until thoroughly moist. It is then left until the compost has almost dried right out before watering again. This is

particularly important during winter and at lower temperatures.

Feeding: Once a month between March and September. None during winter.

Special points: These remarkable ferns attract attention on account of the fertile fronds that dangle from the centre of the plant. Reminiscent of stag's head trophies in hunting lodges and ancestral homes, they give rise to the common names. *Platycerium bifurcatum*, from eastern Australia to Polynesia, is the most commonly grown. I grew a plant for years in an unheated bedroom about 3 feet (1 metre) from an east-facing window. *Platycerium grande* will grow enormous. In normal room conditions, due to lack of humidity, the sterile (wrapping) fronds may not stay green and grow as large as they should. Fertile fronds sometimes produce spores on their undersides. These can be tapped on to paper and sown (see p. 14).

PLECTRANTHUS

Common name: candle plant, Swedish ivy

Position: Good light with some direct light is necessary for satisfactory growth. *P. oertendahlii* (candle plant) can tolerate less light but becomes straggly. Normal room temperatures of 60 to 70°F (15 to 21°C) are ideal. Lower temperatures are tolerated but below 50°F (10°C) plants will begin to suffer. Avoid fluctuations which can lead to

Plectranthus coleoides 'Marginatus'

leaf drop. *P. coleoides* is particularly sensitive.

Watering: Strongly growing plants require a lot of water as they have very active root systems. Never leave standing in water and take care over newly potted plants and those over-wintering at lower temperatures. This means allowing the surface of the compost to begin to dry out before the next watering.

Feeding: From March, when plants are growing strongly, feed fortnightly. During winter every six weeks is adequate.

Special points: The most commonly grown plectranthus would seem to be *P. oertendahlii* with its rounded, rather pale leaves and often reddish stems if grown in good light. My favourite is *P. coleoides* 'Marginatus' with fleshy, aromatic, cream-edged leaves. Both these grow well in a

hanging basket, well watered, in good light and a steady, warm temperature. Shoot-tip cuttings root easily. As they grow, pinch the tips out to encourage bushy plants.

PRIMULA ✳ ☼ Ⓑ

Position: Good, direct light is needed. Sometimes the bright light experienced on a south- or west-facing windowsill might scorch the plant. A cool temperature between 50 and 55°F (10 to 13°C) is ideal. Down to 40°F (5°C) is tolerated by most and *Primula obconica* can tolerate slightly higher temperatures without too much suffering. Over 60°F (15°C) plants will very

Primula malacoides

quickly go off. The worst position is a warm, dark place. The best is a bright, cool room close to a window.

Watering: Allow the surface of the compost to just begin to dry out between waterings. The bulk of the compost should never dry out but do not leave the pot standing in water.

Feeding: Fortnightly during summer. During winter they may still be actively growing and flowering and will need regular feeds. However, at low temperatures watering will be reduced, so reduce the feed to every three or four weeks.

Special points: An excellent group of

Primula obconica

flowering house plants, they can be long-lasting. Perhaps the most popular is *P. obconica*, which will flower almost continuously for at least two years if well looked after. The hairy leaves can give some people a rash, especially on the insides of the arms and on the face, so take care when handling them. *Primula sinensis* is rather similar in appearance but has a prettier leaf and is not often seen for sale. Neither, unfortunately, is the long-lasting *P.* × *kewensis* which has a bright yellow flower. The leaves and stalks are often coated with whitish powder. *Primula malacoides* is freely available and a fine, dainty plant with many flowers. This is not as long lasting as the others. Plants are propagated by seed, surface sown on to seed compost (see pp. 13–14).

PTERIS

Common name: brake fern, ribbon fern
Position: Good light but not direct sunlight which might scorch the delicate fronds. A temperature of 60 to 65°F (15 to 18°C) is ideal. Above this, humidity must be raised by grouping the fern with other plants or standing on a tray of moist pebbles. *Pteris cretica*, the most popular ribbon fern, is not very happy under 50 to 55°F (10 to 13°C).
Watering: Keep moist but do not stand in water.
Feeding: When ferns are growing actively, producing new fronds from the centre, then

Pteris ensiformis 'Evergemiensis'

ferns to plant up in bowls with other plants. Propagation is by dividing plants when they become large. Spores can be collected from plants or bought. They are usually included in spore mixtures of indoor ferns (see p. 14 for sowing).

RADERMACHERA

Position: Good light is necessary for con- tinued growth. Plants thrive at tempera- tures of 55 to 70°F (13 to 21°C), providing they are steady, not fluctuating.

Watering: Allow the surface of the com- post to dry out before watering again. Casualties are probably due to a combina- tion of not enough light and over-watering.

Feeding: While plants are showing signs

feed fortnightly during summer and monthly during winter with a well-balanced liquid feed.

Special points: These are attractive, deli- cate-looking ferns most popularly repre- sented by smaller, variegated types of *Pteris cretica* and the crested types with compli- cated, frilly fronds looking as though they are exploding into fresh growth at the tips. The variegated kinds definitely need good light. As an experiment I tried one in a dingy hallway. Although it did not die, it certainly stopped growing and almost seemed to shrink. The larger, plain green kinds are bet- ter able to tolerate low light. They are good

Radermachera sinica

of active growth, encourage them by fort-nightly feeds.

Special points: *Radermachera sinica* is a relatively recent house plant introduction deriving from India, China, the Philippines and Java. Initially called *Stereospermum sinicum*, they would grow to small trees in the wild. When mature they bear yellow, trumpet-shaped blooms, which is not surprising as they belong to the same family as trumpet vines and catalpas. Flowers have never, to my knowledge, been produced in home or conservatory, the plants being grown purely as small shrubs for their attractive foliage. Although they do not require high temperatures, they appear to be vulnerable to sudden temperature changes and draughts. Couple these problems with over-watering and you soon have a dead plant on your hands. Spindly plants can be pruned back in spring and stood in a bright position to encourage healthy regrowth. Propagation is usually by seed.

RHODODENDRON ☼

Common name: azalea
Position: Good light with some direct light. Harsh light from south- or west-facing windows is too bright. My plant does well just 2 feet (60 cm) away from east-facing French doors. I have also seen some fine plants in a sunny hallway receiving light from a window and glass door. Good plants for a porch as they also appreciate cool tem-

peratures. The preferred range is 40 to 60°F (5 to 15°C). At high temperatures the air is too dry, flowers go over fast, the compost dries out too quickly and new shoots become long and drawn.

Watering: These plants must be kept moist. They are bought crammed tightly into a peat-based compost which dries very fast. Often there is not sufficient space at the top for watering. Once plants have flagged once or twice their health and development will be damaged. My advice is to stand them in a large, high-sided container so that they can be watered from top and bottom. Do remember to tip away any excess after a few hours. They are acid-loving plants and dislike hard, limy water. Collect rainwater if your tap water is hard.

Rhododendron

Should you be forced into using hard tap water, then use a liquid feed for acid-loving plants at half strength for every watering.

Feeding: Even when using soft water it will be beneficial to feed the plants every fortnight from the time the flowers fade to late autumn. This will help the strength of the growth that is made during this period. Again, use a fertiliser for acid-lovers.

Special points: Azaleas are now grouped together with *Rhododendron*. As they are often pot-bound when bought, wait until flowering has finished, then repot using a compost for acid-loving plants. The new pot should be two sizes larger (for example, a 4-inch (10-cm) to a 6-inch (15-cm) pot). Keep in a light, cool place until there is no danger of frost. The plant can then be stood outside in a semi-shady spot. If your garden soil is acid the pot can be plunged into the soil. Keep watered and feed well until autumn. Bring indoors again before there is any danger of frost and carry on as before. Tip cuttings can be taken from new growths in spring.

SAINTPAULIA

Common name: African violet

Position: Good light is essential but avoid direct, scorching light which will damage the plants. A window shaded by a net curtain is often a good position. Some of my best plants flourish a short distance away from an east-facing window where they receive some morning sunshine but not midday or afternoon sun. The other advantage of this position is the radiator under the window which keeps a high temperature. Unfortunately the temperature at night usually drops close to a window, where most plants are placed for the light. This fluctuation is sufficient to stop plants flowering. A double-glazed window is ideal. A constant temperature of 65 to 70°F (18 to 21°C) is preferred. Above this, some provision for humidity must be made, perhaps by standing the plant on a tray of moist pebbles. Below 60°F (15°C) plants stay alive but seem to stop growing and flowering. The people who seem to have the secret of making them flower are not so much gifted with green fingers as ideal room conditions.

Watering: As the plants like to be warm, to give them cold water straight from the tap is a great shock. Allow water to stand until it reaches room temperature, or, if pushed, add a little warm water. Watering from above can cause the crown or centre of the plant to rot. Stand the plants in saucers large enough to hold water which can be taken up from below. After a couple of hours any excess water should be thrown away. The surface of the compost should be allowed to dry out so that the leaves of the plant are just beginning to go down before another watering is given.

Feeding: Buy a liquid fertiliser specially formulated for African violets for the best results. Add this to the water every two

Saintpaulia

SANSEVIERIA ☐ ✿ B

Common name: mother-in-law's tongue
Position: Good light is necessary. They like full sun but can also tolerate some shade, for example the sun filtered through net curtains or by a north-facing window. They will continue to stay alive in the shade but will stop growing, and become prone to over-watering. Normal room temperatures of 65 to 70°F (18 to 21°C) are ideal but they can tolerate much lower temperatures, down to 40°F (5°C). At lower temperatures great care must be taken not to over-water.

weeks during summer, and monthly in winter if plants are still growing.
Special points: There are many named cultivars of different colours, shapes and sizes. A collection of miniatures have been bred from *Saintpaulia pusilla* which would hardly take up any space at all. Propagation is by leaf cuttings which can be rooted in water (see pp. 17–18). The best plants are those that just have one crown or rosette of growth. Sometimes, having successfully rooted a cutting, a cluster of small plants develops. These are best separated when still young. A light, peaty compost is ideal. Ordinary multi-purpose composts are acceptable but there are special African violet composts for the enthusiast. If you really get bitten by the saintpaulia bug, then join the Saintpaulia and Houseplant Society (see p. 126).

Watering: Treat sansevierias like succulent plants. During winter when light is poor they will hardly grow and can be kept very much on the dry side. Between March and October they can be watered regularly, allowing the surface of the compost to dry out in between.
Feeding: Give a well-balanced liquid feed fortnightly between March and October.
Special points: These plants are extremely tough and accommodating provided they are not over-watered. A large group, mostly originating from South Africa, they are represented in cultivation by *Sansevieria trifasciata*, in particular the form 'Laurentii' which has the familiar yellow stripe down the edges of the leaves. You might also find squat little plants, now seen as another form called 'Hahnii'. Spikes of small, greenish-white flowers are sometimes produced on

Sansevieria trifasciata 'Laurentii'

happy plants grown in a bright place. A viewer of *Gardeners' World* once wrote to tell me that these are scented in the evening. I have found that these plants prefer a loam-based compost with a little added peat and sharp sand. At potting time, in the spring, they can be divided. This sometimes involves cutting through underground stems to separate two clumps. Another method of propagation involves leaf cuttings. Take off a healthy leaf nearing maturity and cut across into sections 3 inches (7.5 cm) long. Insert these, upright, into cutting compost (equal parts of peat and

sharp sand or vermiculite). Do not cover, keep out of full sun and roots will grow from the base followed by new plants. However, if this is carried out on the form 'Laurentii' you will lose the yellow margin in the offspring.

SAXIFRAGA ☼ B

Common name: mother-of-thousands
Position: Good light with some direct light each day. Normal room temperatures of 60 to 70°F (15 to 21°C) are a little too warm for these cool-loving plants. A better temperature range is 40 to 60°F (5 to 15°C). My plant has grown large and fine in an unheated, west-facing porch. During very cold spells I move the plant into the house to keep it above freezing.
Watering: Allow the surface to begin drying out between waterings. This is

Saxifraga stolonifera

particularly important during cold winter spells.

Feeding: While actively growing, liquid feed fortnightly.

Special points: *Saxifraga stolonifera* (used to be *S. sarmentosa*) is an old-fashioned house plant but an attractive one, grown mainly for its foliage. Long flower stalks bearing small white flowers appear during late spring. The characteristic that gives the plant its common name is the bearing of plantlets on runners, rather like a strawberry plant. I let my plants grow large, potting them on without dividing them, so that all the runners tumble over the sides. When they become choked in the pot, then divide up or replace with young plants grown from the runners. This is easily done by snipping the small plants off and potting them separately. *S.s.* 'Tricolor' is a smaller-leaved form with pink, green and cream leaves.

SCHEFFLERA ☐

Common name: parasol plant
Position: Good light but too much strong light will scorch or bleach the foliage. Normal room temperatures of 60 to 70°F (15 to 21°C) are ideal. Plants can survive much lower temperatures without dying but will refuse to grow properly under about 50°F (10°C).
Watering: Allow the surface of the compost time to dry out between waterings.
Feeding: While showing signs of active growth, feed fortnightly during summer but just monthly during winter.

Special points: *Schefflera (Heptapleurum) arboricola* is a popular house plant. Sometimes a pot holding four or more plants trained up a central moss pole or stake to 5 or 6 feet (about a metre and a half) in height is sold as a specimen plant to rival tall weeping figs. However, like weeping figs, they are not easy to keep healthy. A constant, warm temperature without fluctuations, provision for extra humidity if the air is dry, and a position in good light are necessary to maintain the quality of plant you have bought. Try and remember to turn the plant regularly so

Schefflera arboricola

that all sides receive light. Smaller plants tend to have single stems and become rather tall and spindly. Tie in to a stake to keep the main stem straight. A very straggly plant can be pruned in spring. Kept in a light place it should sprout new stems. Cutting the tops out of small plants can encourage a bushy form rather than a straight stem. The tips can be rooted as cuttings. There is a variegated form and some with slightly different leaflet colours and shape.

SCHLUMBERGERA

Common name: Christmas cactus, Easter cactus

Position: Good light is necessary for strong growth and flowering. Too much bright light will cause yellowing and ill-health. Temperatures of 60 to 65°F (15 to 18°C) are suitable. However, lower temperatures down to 40°F (5°C) are tolerated.

Watering: During spring and summer, keep the compost moist without allowing water to sit in the saucer. During winter, leading up to and during flowering, allow the surface of the compost time to begin to dry out between waterings. However, once plants have flowered keep them just a bit drier until spring arrives and growth becomes active again.

Feeding: Use a high-potash liquid feed fortnightly from March until the flower buds have formed.

Special points: Although cacti, *Schlumbergera* come from tropical Brazil and live epiphytically in pockets of decayed matter which form in the branches of trees. As such they do not want or need very bright light and like a warmer temperature, more water and humidity than their desert counterparts. Most of the plants grown are hybrids between two or three species, the best known being *Schlumbergera* (which used to be called *Zygocactus*) *truncata*. These hybrids flower at all sorts of different times through winter and early spring. They also have an exciting colour range of whites, reds and pinks. They are 'short day' plants (the shorter days of winter tell them to start initiating flower buds) and sometimes refuse to flower if they are exposed to too much artificial light. Once buds have formed, avoid moving the plants as in turning back

Schlumbergera

towards the light the buds might drop off. Cuttings consisting of two to three segments are easy to root in spring. Providing you remember to water them, a spell in the garden during summer will often help them to flower well the following winter.

SCILLA ✳ ☼

Common name: wood-hyacinth
Position: Very good light is needed for strong growth. A porch or sunny window-sill is ideal. Cool temperatures between 40 and 50°F (5 and 10°C) are preferred to ordinary room temperatures. Do not allow the temperature to go below freezing.
Watering: Allow the surface time to dry out between watering. At low temperatures during winter, this means that there will be

Scilla socialis 'Violacea'

long gaps between waterings.
Feeding: Monthly between March and October with a well-balanced liquid feed.
Special points: These are house plants that are rarely seen for sale, yet are spread around between keen house plant growers who often have no idea what the plant is called. *Scilla violacea*, *Scilla socialis* 'Violacea' or *Ledebouria violacea* are all correct names. Of South African origin, the bulbous plants make an attractive potful with their spotted leaves and spikes of pale violet flowers in spring. A John Innes No. 2 with added peat and sharp sand is a good compost. A clay pan, shallower than an ordinary pot, is the most suitable and attractive container. Propagation is by division of the clump after flowering.

SCINDAPSUS ☐ ☼ Ⓑ ●

Common name: devil's ivy
Position: Plants grow best in good but not direct light. They can grow in low light but leaves become smaller and colours less bright. My own plant trails around a small table about 10 feet (3 metres) from an east-facing window. Normal room temperatures are acceptable but they can tolerate a minimum of 50°F (10°C).
Watering: Allow the surface of the compost time to dry out between waterings.
Feedings: Give a well-balanced liquid feed every two weeks during summer, but just a couple of times during winter.

Scindapsus aureus

Special points: These foliage house plants from the Solomon Islands are easy to grow and will adapt to a wide range of room conditions. Trained up a moss pole they will climb, but left to their own devices they will trail most attractively. *Scindapsus aureus* has been called *Raphidophora* and, more correctly, *Epipremnum*. However, as the house plant trade still refers to them as *Scindapsus*, this is the most useful name to remember.

Dust leaves frequently so that light can reach the leaf. Long stems that become a nuisance can be pruned back by cutting just beyond a leaf. A new shoot will grow from just past the last leaf on the stem. Propagation is simply by taking shoot-tip cuttings 3 inches (7.5 cm) long. Alternatively, one can capitalise on long lengths of stem by cutting below a lower leaf and above an upper one to create a cutting with no growing tip but containing two nodes. Remove the bottom leaf, insert several of these into a small pot of cutting compost, keep warm, moist and out of direct light and roots soon form. A new shoot will grow from between the axil of the upper leaf and the stem. Pot three cuttings up together to create a more instant effect.

SCIRPUS

Common name: rush. I call it the fibre-optics plant.
Position: Medium light is adequate. My own plant thrives 9 or 10 feet (about 3 metres) away from an east-facing window. Normal room temperatures of 60 to 65°F (15 to 18°C) are acceptable but lower temperatures down to 45°F (7°C) are tolerated.
Watering: These plants grow in wet places naturally and so can tolerate being constantly moist at the roots when they are growing strongly. During winter, especially when temperatures are low, allow the surface of the compost to dry out slightly between waterings.

Feeding: Give a well-balanced liquid feed monthly in summer but just once or twice during winter.

Special points: These are attractive plants with trailing leaves tipped with tiny cream-coloured flowers. They look good in hanging baskets for the porch or conservatory and trail attractively over the edges of shelves and mantels. I would never buy one of those awful plants that appear to be growing out of a tube, as I think they look most unnatural and would be more difficult to look after. Propagation is by dividing the clump of leaves carefully apart into smaller groups which are then potted separately into small pots. Water very carefully as the young plant grows roots down into the new compost, as they should not be too wet at this stage.

Scirpus cernuus

SELAGINELLA ✿ ●

Position: As their mossy appearance suggests, these plants like a shady spot. However, there must be some light for growth. The most important condition is humidity which seems vital to their well-being. Temperatures of 60 to 70°F (15 to 21°C) are ideal as long as dry air can be avoided. These are excellent plants for bottle gardens and terraria. The best colony I ever saw was planted up in an old fish tank.

Watering: Although needing to be kept moist, these delicate plants should not be continuously saturated so that the surface of the compost begins to dry just slightly between waterings. As they tend to fill the pot with a mound of foliage, watering is best done from below. Do not leave water in the saucer after sufficient has been taken up.

Feeding: A well-balanced liquid feed at half strength, given monthly, is adequate.

Special points: These plants respond to cosseting. They must be kept humid by grouping together or with other plants. Misting them lightly with water at room temperature will be appreciated. Never allow them to dry out at the roots but if saturated they will quickly rot. In a bottle garden they will need a shady spot so that the temperature inside does not rise too high as this, too, will result in the plant rotting. *Selaginella kraussiana* 'Brownii' is one of the finest and most popular, its tiny crinkled leaves resembling fine parsley. *S. k.*

Selaginella martensii 'Watsoniana' (left), S. kraussiana 'Brownii' (right)

'Aurea' is larger with golden leaves. Tougher and large is *S. martensii*, which produces stilt-like roots. *S.m.* 'Variegata' has silvery-white tips to the leaves. A very attractive bowl can be made up by planting several different selaginellas together, but take great care of them. Propagation is by taking small cuttings 2 inches (5 cm) long.

SOLANUM

Common name: winter cherry
Position: Good light is needed for balanced growth. Once plants are in berry they can be placed away from a window. My own plant stays fresh for long periods on a sideboard facing, but 10 feet (3 metres) away from, an east-facing window. The cooler the room you can give them, the longer these plants will last in berry. Minimum would be 40°F (5°C), ideal 55°F (13°C) and maximum 60°F (15°C).

Watering: Allow the surface of the compost just to dry out between waterings.

Feeding: Give fortnightly liquid feeds at any time of the year when plants are actively growing. A high-potash fertiliser will encourage flowers and fruiting on plants being grown on for a second or more years. At low temperatures where less water needs to be given, reduce feeds to every month.

Special points: *Solanum capsicastrum* is a Brazilian plant grown for its showy orange-red berries produced and lasting all winter. Those with a greenhouse can raise their own plants from spring-sown seed but most house plant growers buy their plants already

Solanum capsicastrum

in berry during the autumn. Look after your plant well and it can be kept over for another year. When all danger of frost is past, prune back about two-thirds of the growth and stand the plant outside for the summer, during which time it will produce small white flowers. Tap the stems and occasionally mist-spray to assist pollination and the berries will form. Bring back indoors before the first frosts. Although *Solanum* is related to tomatoes and potatoes, the fruits are not edible.

Soleirolia soleirolii

SOLEIROLIA

Common name: mind-your-own-business, baby's tears

Position: Plants seem able to grow well in bright or shady spots. The first plant I ever kept lived in the shady corner of a bright room but the plant I now grow lives well in a bright, west-facing porch. A cool room is preferable. Plants can tolerate temperatures almost down to freezing but would have difficulty in temperatures much above 60°F (15°C).

Watering: Plants should not be allowed to dry out to the point of flagging but to sit in water would lead to the plant rotting away. Always water from the bottom, as pouring water on to the mound of small leaves will also cause rotting. Any excess water should be tipped away after an hour or so.

Feeding: A well-balanced liquid feed given every three weeks in summer but just a couple of times during winter will be much appreciated.

Special points: Some people have problems controlling *Soleirolia soleirolii*, a native of Corsica and Sardinia, as it frequently grows as a weed in moist parts of the garden, even infesting lawns. However, it does make a most attractive house plant as a large mound of foliage. My own plant is huge and sits on a pedestal in the west-facing porch where it gains much attention. Tiny white flowers are rather insignificant. There are golden and silver forms to choose from although they are less robust and, in my opinion, less attractive. To take cuttings I usually pull off a tuft of growth about 2 inches (5 cm) long and insert it as a clump into cutting compost.

SPATHIPHYLLUM * □ Ⓑ

Common name: peace lily

Position: Good light is needed for healthy growth and flower production. Plants can tolerate a shady spot but growth will slow down and flower production stop. The bright light of a south- or west-facing window is too harsh and might scorch. My own plant thrives standing to one side of east-facing French doors. Normal room temperatures of 60 to 70°F (15 to 21°C) are ideal. A minimum of 50°F (10°C) will be toler-

ated but plants remain stunted and growth slow.

Watering: Allow the surface of the compost time to dry out between waterings, especially if asked to grow at low temperatures.

Feeding: Give a well-balanced liquid feed fortnightly during summer but just monthly if growing at warm temperatures during winter.

Special points: *Spathiphyllum wallisii*, from Colombia and Venezuela, makes a beautiful house plant with attractive leaves and flowers like dainty arum lilies, to which they are related. Recently, hybrids have been taking over from the rather diminutive species, first the larger 'Mauna Loa' and now even larger hybrids, giving plants up to 3 feet (1 metre) in height. Plants will do best in a warm room, in good light, not over-watered, and stood on a tray of moist pebbles to raise humidity. Propagation is by division.

Spathiphyllum

STEPHANOTIS

Common name: Madagascar jasmine

Position: Good light is needed for reliable flowering. Bright summer sunshine coming through a south-facing window might scorch the foliage. A steady, warm temperature of 65 to 70°F (18 to 21°C) is ideal for flowering. They dislike fluctuations and are really suitable for bright houses with double glazing so they can stand near a window without draughts.

Watering: Allow the surface of the compost time to dry out between waterings.

Feeding: Give a well-balanced liquid feed fortnightly during summer and just once or twice during winter.

Special points: These plants can have an infuriating habit of refusing to flower. Light and warmth are the key to success here. You are less likely to fail through lack of skill than by just not having suitable room conditions. Plants can be trained round a circular wire but seem to do better if they can be given a bit of headroom. Try making a tripod of tall canes for them, or grow up a trellis. *Stephanotis floribunda* is attractive even when not

Stephanotis floribunda

flowering for its glossy green leaves. The flowers are creamy-white, waxy and have a delicious perfume. Those successful in getting plants to flower might find that their plants produce enormous, egg-shaped fruits. These will take up to a year to become ripe and eventually split open, releasing small seeds each with a silky parasol of fine hairs, presumably for wind dispersal. Of course, these can be sown and grown on into new plants. The more conventional method of propagation is by 3 to 4 inch (7.5 to 10 cm) long shoot-tip cuttings.

STREPTOCARPUS * □

Common name: Cape primrose

Position: Good but not direct light. Temperatures of 60 to 70°F (15 to 21°C) are ideal. Below 60°F (15°C) flower buds stop forming and at higher temperatures provision must be made to increase humidity. Do not spray the foliage but stand plants on a tray of moist gravel instead.

Watering: Allow the surface of the compost time to dry out between waterings. Water from the bottom but do not allow plants to stand in water for longer than an hour.

Feeding: Give a high-potash liquid feed fortnightly during summer but monthly during winter. At lower temperatures, if plants are having a rest period, do not feed at all.

Special points: These are lovely plants with hairy leaves and exotic flowers which

Streptocarpus

can be produced almost non-stop in the right conditions. New stock can be ordered from specialist nurseries (see p. 126 for stockists). In this way young, named varieties can be obtained in many different flower colours. The large leaves will become dusty indoors and can be cleaned with a soft brush. As plants grow older they become choked with leaves and not so inclined to flower. This is the time to select a healthy leaf at the peak of its development to use for leaf cuttings (see pp. 19–20).

SUCCULENTS ☐ ☼

Position: These need maximum light. A position close to a window is essential. Normal room temperatures are acceptable, although most will tolerate temperatures down to 40°F (5°C) during their winter rest.

Watering: Like cacti, most succulent plants have an ability to store water and withstand a certain amount of drought. However, this is not an excuse to neglect these plants as is so often the case. During winter, they will only need a few good waterings to prevent them from shrivelling. At cool temperatures they will hardly need any water at all. By March they will be ready for a good soak, and thereafter regular watering, just allowing the top couple of inches (5 cm) of compost time to dry out between waterings.

Feeding: None in winter. Every month with a liquid feed for cacti and succulents between March and October.

Special points: Succulents make most attractive house plants when well looked after. So often they are represented by a couple of starving, pot-bound *Aloe aristata*. There is *Senecio rowleyanus* with long strands of growth that look just like a necklace of round beads, *Aichryson* with their rosettes of fleshy leaves and yellow flowers, *Echeveria*, *Stapelia* with succulent stems and smelly flowers like tapestry, *Kleinia*, often called candle cactus, which has its growth period in the winter instead of the summer, and many more. Potting compost for these plants should be similar to that described for cacti – well drained and gritty. Adding extra grit or sharp sand to a John Innes No. 2 is an easy way of achieving this. Propagation of those plants that have distinct rosettes of growth can be by division. Others have

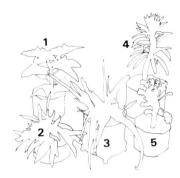

Succulents:
1 *Kalanchoe beharensis*
2 *Glottiphyllum longum*
3 *Aloe burgersfortensis*
4 *Senecio kleinia*
5 *Pelargonium klinghardtense*

definite stems and leaves so that ordinary cuttings can be made. *Sedum, Echeveria, Crassula* and others whose leaves come away easily can often be propagated by leaf cuttings. Push the base of a detached leaf into cutting compost (equal amounts of sharp sand and peat). Leave dry for two to three days before watering in. Allow the compost to dry out between waterings and do not cover.

SYNGONIUM □

Common name: goosefoot plant, arrowhead

Position: Good light is needed for strong growth. Keep out of direct light which might scorch. Normal room temperatures of 65 to 70°F (18 to 21°C) are ideal. Increase humidity by grouping with other plants or standing on a saucer of moist pebbles. Plants will not thrive at temperatures constantly dipping to 55°F (13°C) or below.

Watering: Allow the surface of the compost time to dry out between waterings.

Feeding: Give a well-balanced liquid feed fortnightly during summer but monthly during winter only if plants are still showing signs of active growth.

Special points: *Syngonium podophyllum* will remain a compact, rounded plant until it begins to mature, when it starts to climb or trail. However, plants will only become rampant if they are given ideal conditions of light, warmth and humidity, rarely found in ordinary houses. Nevertheless, they are charming foliage plants and make nice additions to planted bowls of similar tropical plants. Propagation is by tip cuttings 3 to 4 inches (7.5 to 10 cm) long.

Syngonium

TILLANDSIA

Common name: Some are called air plants.

Position: Good light is needed for strong, healthy growth but this light must be filtered or from a north- or east-facing window to avoid scorching or excessive drying out. A temperature of 60 to 65°F (15 to 18°C) suits them best. Above this the air is usually too dry and misting must be frequent. Most do not grow well below 50°F (10°C).

Watering: The larger species growing in pots have a restricted root system and so need careful watering. They will not need watering as regularly as other kinds of house plants. Wait until you can no longer squeeze moisture in the surface of the compost before watering again. Do not leave standing in water. The air plant types which are fixed to bark or some other ornament need misting lightly. This should be done at least daily during summer and if the air is hot and dry during winter too. During cold, damp spells, mist perhaps only two or three times a week. Ideally the water should have dried from the plants within two to three hours. If they remain wet and the atmosphere is cold and damp they will quickly rot away. If they are left dry too long in a hot, dry atmosphere they will gradually shrivel up and die.

Feeding: Give a half-strength foliar feed every two months.

Special points: My favourite is *Tillandsia cyanea*, a compact plant from Guatemala which would live up in the trees, clinging to a niche in bark or tree limbs. A large pink bract is produced from which bright, purplish-blue flowers are formed, usually one by one, over a long period. Having performed, the rosette which produced the bract will very slowly die off, but numerous offsets grow up around it to take over. Under ideal conditions colonies will become quite large. *Tillandsia usneoides* is another favourite, often called Spanish moss. The greyish-silver skeins of growth are hundreds of tiny little plants linked together. Scaly leaves act like blotting paper to absorb their water and nourishment, literally, from the air. I have found these and other air-plant tillandsias which do not

grow in pots difficult to grow indoors as they need careful attention.

TOLMIEA ✿ B

Common name: mother of thousands, pick-a-back plant

Position: Good light is needed for healthy growth. This is particularly important for the variegated form. Normal room temperatures of 60 to 65°F (15 to 18°C) are suitable. However, lower temperatures almost down to freezing will be tolerated. A minimum for a good, healthy plant would be 40°F (5°C).

Watering: Never leave standing in water. Allow the surface of the compost time to dry out between waterings. At low winter temperatures the compost can be kept much drier.

Feeding: Fortnightly liquid feeds during

Tolmiea menziesii 'Variegata'

summer but just a couple of feeds during winter, only if the plants are growing at high temperatures.

Special points: These are attractive foliage plants which make a compact potful of growth. Once leaves have matured, a small plant will grow from the portion of leaf as it joins its stalk, giving rise to the common names. While adding to the attractiveness of the plant, these 'mother leaves' can also be taken off the plant and used for propagation. Leave a small stalk on the leaf, which anchors it into the cutting compost, ensuring close contact between leaf and compost. After a few weeks the plantlet will have roots of its own and begin to grow when it can be potted up. Eventually the mother leaf withers away.

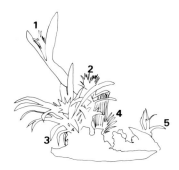

Tillandsia arrangement:
1 and **2** *T. ionantha*
3 *Guzmania 'Minor Red'*
4 *T. juncea*
5 *T. caput-medusae*

TRADESCANTIA ☼ B

Common name: wandering Jew
Position: Good light is needed for strong growth. Too much light leads to bleaching and scorching of leaves, too little to spindly growth and leaves losing their attractive colourings. Cool to normal room temperatures are appreciated. A temperature of 55 to 60°F (13 to 15°C) is optimum. Down to 50°F (10°C) will be tolerated, but at higher temperatures plants tend to suffer from brown tips to the leaves.
Watering: When growing strongly, keep the compost moist, although do not leave

standing in water. At lower temperatures during periods when growth stops, allow the surface to dry out between waterings.
Feeding: Liquid feed fortnightly during summer but just a couple of times throughout winter if plants are growing in warm rooms.
Special points: There are many different types of tradescantia which make easy-to-grow, trailing house plants. Those with soft or fleshy leaves like *T. blossfeldiana* which has dark leaves, purple on the undersides, and *T. sillamontana* with its pale green, soft, hairy leaves, need more careful watering than the types with thinner leaves. All will become scruffy with time and need to be pruned back when this happens. Sometimes, as in the case of *T. sillamontana*, you will see lots of new growth appearing at the base which is a good sign to cut off all the old. With others, simply decide to give them a haircut, in spring or summer, trimming off all growth to within about 2 to 3 inches (5 to 7.5 cm) of the base. New growth quickly takes over. Cuttings of thin-leaved types root well in water, while those with stiffer leaves prefer to root in cutting compost. Make cuttings 2 to 3 inches (5 to 7.5 cm) long. When rooted, pot them three or four to one pot and after a couple of weeks pinch the tips out to encourage branching.

Tradescantia fluminensis 'Rochfords Quicksilver' (back),
T. fluminensis 'Variegata' (front)

YUCCA ☐ ☼ Ⓑ ●

Position: Good light, with some direct sunshine each day, is necessary for healthy growth. If placed in a dark corner they will not die but simply stop growing. Normal room temperatures of 60 to 70°F (15 to 21°C) are appreciated but temperatures as low as 50°F (10°C) will also give good results. During winter, plants almost prefer to be a little cooler if they are not in good light, otherwise they struggle to grow, producing spindly pale-green leaves. These plants are very tolerant of dry air.

Watering: During summer, when plants are growing strongly, keep moist. During rest periods, at lower temperatures when growth has stopped, allow the compost to become quite dry between waterings.

Feeding: Give a well-balanced liquid feed fortnightly during periods of strong growth only.

Yucca elephantipes

Special points: These have never been my favourite house plants although there was a recent craze for them. They do have the advantage of being able to tolerate hot, dry air, making them most suitable for modern homes and offices. It is possible to buy plants as stumpy pieces of stem which are stood in water to produce roots before being potted, but you need a lot of patience. The most practical method for propagation is to cut sideshoots away from the parent plant and insert them into a pot of cutting compost. Keep very much on the dry side, and after several months roots should have formed. This is best done in spring so that the plant has the whole summer to get going. Tall, overgrown yuccas can be pruned back. If stood in a light spot they will usually break into new growth. Plants will benefit from a summer break in the garden.

ZEBRINA ☼ B

Common name: wandering Jew
Position: Good, direct light is necessary to keep the interesting leaf colours. Normal room temperatures of 60 to 70°F (15 to 21°C) are ideal. Temperatures down to 50°F (10°C) can be tolerated.
Watering: Allow the surface of the compost time to dry out between waterings.
Feeding: Every fortnight during summer with a well-balanced liquid feed. Just a couple of times during winter if grown in a warm room.
Special points: *Zebrina pendula* is, as the name suggests, a plant with a striped leaf. Trailing in nature and very similar to its close relative, *Tradescantia*, the leaves are striped with silver. Straggly plants should be cut back hard, in spring or summer, to within 2 to 3 inches (5 to 7.5 cm) of the base to promote new growth. Select shoot tips with the best leaf colours to use as cutting material. These, 3 inches (7.5 cm) long, will root either in water or cutting compost. Pot up three to a pot and pinch back to get a bushy effect.

Zebrina pendula

3

TROUBLE SHOOTER

PEST PROBLEMS

Small attacks of house plant pests are usually easy to deal with if they are spotted early enough. Inspect plants regularly and learn to recognise the tell-tale signs of pest damage. Identify the culprits and set about controlling them before they breed into plague proportions. Most controls take the shape of pesticides applied as sprays. If you are an organic gardener determined to extend your philosophy to indoor plants, then there are organic alternatives available. Systemic controls can be applied to the plant by spraying or by pushing tabs or sticks into the compost. The plant takes the chemicals up so that when the pest sucks its sap it takes in a dose, which hopefully will kill it. Always follow instructions carefully to ensure that products are applied safely and effectively.

APHIDS

These are commonly referred to as greenfly and blackfly, usually attacking soft, sappy shoots, new leaves and flower buds. Sticky patches on the plant are a warning sign. Fortunately they are relatively easy to kill.

Aphids are a nuisance, sucking sap from leaves, new shoots and buds. Spotted early enough, they should be easy to control.

WHITEFLY

Small white flies, eggs and scales are found on the undersides of leaves. On tapping the plant the adults will fly off like a cloud around the plant. Sticky honeydew falls on to lower leaves making a mess and often causing growth of sooty mould which looks like a black, sooty powder on the leaf surface. Fortunately whitefly is more a pest of greenhouse than house. Plants like *Fuchsia*, *Beloperone* (shrimp plant) and *Hibiscus* might be affected.

Small white flies, eggs and scales on the undersides of leaves are sure signs of whitefly.

Right: It is important to spot the tell-tale signs of red spider mite before they get this bad. Leaves become speckled and scorched-looking.

RED SPIDER MITE

These are among the worst house plant pests as they are difficult to spot until they have reached plague proportions. Signs to watch out for are tiny speckles on leaves which begin to look rather dried out. Suspect leaves should be examined on the undersides, with a magnifying glass if necessary. Red spider mite is a bit of a misnomer as they are more of a fawn colour, often with two black dots. Plants often infested include *Aspidistra*, *Impatiens*, *Calathea* and palms. Dry air encourages the mites so it is a good idea to increase humidity around susceptible plants. Regular misting under, as well as over, leaves will help. A chemical spray applied just once is not usually sufficient to

give effective control. Should the instructions on the product tell you to repeat the spray after a number of days, make sure you do this, to catch the successive generations of mites as they hatch out of their eggs. Advanced infestations lead to webbing formed around the shoots and leaves of the plant, but by this stage control is very difficult and it is easier to throw the plant away and buy another. Sometimes pruning most of the growth and mites off the plant will work. Stand the plant in a light place and it will sprout new shoots which you can spray or treat with a soil-applied systemic to prevent re-infestation.

MEALY BUG

Again, it is crucial to spot and start controlling these nasty pests before they spread. They are flat, pale-pinkish bugs that suck sap and surround themselves with white waxy powder and filaments which look like wool. Their eggs are also found under this protective coating which makes it difficult for sprays to reach the pests. Small outbreaks can be treated with cotton buds dipped in methylated spirits. Should you need to spray, then make sure you really blast the colonies of bugs to penetrate their mealy protection. Plants often attacked include *Hoya*, *Stephanotis* and *Citrus*. Stickiness is a characteristic of mealy bug attack and often causes sooty mould which feeds on the honeydew they secrete. Root mealy bug works below the soil surface, feeding on

plant roots. Plants looking sad for no reason should be gently tapped out of their pots and examined for any signs of white, powdery mealy bug on the roots. Control in this case consists of drenching the plant in a spray-strength solution of the relevant pesticide.

SCALE

These sap-suckers cover themselves with protective waxy scales which can be white, yellow or dark brown. Sometimes you can see young 'nymphs' crawling off after hatching, to find a new site to colonise. As with other pests, the secretion of honeydew causes stickiness and sooty mould on leaves below. If you see mature scale on plants like *Citrus*, *Ficus* and palms, then clean them off

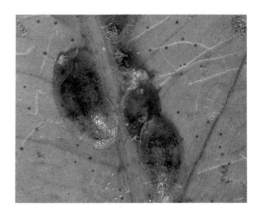

If plant leaves become sticky and show signs of black sooty mould, this could be caused by scale insects which congregate around veins on the leaves.

carefully with soapy water. If the crawling 'nymph' stage are moving about all over the plant then the most effective control would be to spray with the relevant pesticide.

TORTRIX CATERPILLARS

If you grow plants such as begonias and find, one day, that their younger leaves and flowers are stuck together and looking rather nibbled, pull the leaves apart and you might surprise a small caterpillar. These are green or yellow and usually wriggle backwards on discovery. They pull the leaf around themselves with the use of silk webbing and are best controlled by squashing between the fingers (or treading on them, for the squeamish).

PROBLEMS AT THE SURFACE
OF THE COMPOST

I often receive letters from house plant growers who are concerned about activities at the compost surface. The first involves small dark flies which run over and fly up from the compost. These are *Sciarid* flies, also called mushroom flies and fungus gnats. Their larvae, like tiny pale maggots with dark heads, live mostly off rotting matter in the compost. Only occasionally do they attack the roots or stems of plants. They are most rife on continuously moist compost, so try and control the watering better, allowing the surface to become drier between waterings. If you suspect them of causing damage, spray the surface with malathion.

The second problem is when small, wingless insects, like little shrimps or fleas, hop around on the compost surface. These are springtails and also feed off decaying organic matter in the compost. They are less likely to cause damage than *Sciarid* flies. Try replacing the top inch (2 or 3 cm) of compost with large-sized grit or small gravel which might put them off.

FUNGAL ATTACKS

MILDEW

Some house plants, notably *Begonia* and *Cissus rhombifolia* (grape ivy) can suffer from powdery mildew. This manifests itself by a fine white powdery coating over leaves and

You should spot powdery mildew long before it becomes as bad as it is on this *Begonia* leaf.

shoots. These eventually turn yellow, brown and drop off. At the first signs of this, apply the relevant fungicidal spray. This will almost certainly need to be repeated at intervals stated on the instructions. Plants left dry for too long between waterings can be more susceptible.

RUST

Pelargonium rust is the type most likely to be a problem indoors. Round, rusty pustules surrounded by a yellowy patch appear on the undersides of the leaves of zonal pelargoniums. Untreated, the disease will become worse until the whole plant is affected and becomes sick. Keep the foliage of your pelargoniums dry as moisture is needed for rust spores to germinate. At the first signs of attack, remove affected leaves and burn them. Spray plants with the rele-vant fungicide. Rust spores over-winter on leaves. Should you store plants which have been infested indoors during winter for use the following year outside, it might be best to prune back and strip off the leaves. Plants will remain dormant at cool temperatures until the spring.

DAMPING-OFF DISEASE

This is only a problem with seedlings and is a fungal attack which causes seedlings to rot where the stem meets the soil, making them keel over. Do not sow seeds too close, do not over-water seedlings, and if seedlings begin to die off, treat with the relevant fungicide. Should it be necessary to re-sow, take the precaution of drenching the seed compost with the fungicidal solution before sowing, and water seedlings in with the solution after pricking out.

USEFUL ADDRESSES

SEEDS

Chiltern Seeds,
Bortree stile,
Ulverston,
Cumbria LA12 7PB
(0229 581137)

Thompson and Morgan,
London Road,
Ipswich,
Suffolk IP2 0BA
(0473 688588)

PLANTS

The Vernon Geranium Nursery,
Cuddington Way,
Cheam,
Sutton,
Surrey SM2 7JB
(mail order only)

For pelargoniums and ivies:
Fibrex Nurseries Ltd,
Honeybourne Road,
Pebworth,
Nr. Stratford-on-Avon,
Warwick CV37 8XT
(mail order)

For a wide range of palms:
The Palm Centre,
563 Upper Richmond Road West,
London SW14 7ED
(081 876 3223)

For *Streptocarpus* and other gesneriads:
Dibley's Efenechtyd Nurseries,
Cefn Rhydd,
Llanelidan,
Ruthin,
Clwyd LL15 2LG,
North Wales
(097 888 677)
(mail order)

For cacti and succulents:
Holly Gate Cactus Nursery,
Billingshurst Lane,
Ashington,
West Sussex RH20 3BA
(0903 892930)
(mail order)

Carnivorous Plants:
Marston Exotics,
Brampton Lane,
Madley,
Hereford HR2 9LX
(0981 251140)
(mail order)

African Violets:
Tony Clements African Violet Centre,
Station Road,
Terrington St Clement,
King's Lynn,
Norfolk PE34 4PL
(0553 828374)
(mail order)

SOCIETIES

The Saintpaulia and Houseplant Society,
Mrs F. B. F. Dunningham, MBE,
33 Church Road,
Newbury Park,
Ilford,
Essex IG2 7ET

Orchid Society of Great Britain,
Mrs J. Kelleher,
120 Crofton Road,
Orpington,
Kent BR6 8HZ

British Cactus and Succulent Society,
K. Harrow,
23 Linden Leas,
West Wickham,
Kent BR4 0SE

INDEX

Page numbers in *italic* refer to illustrations. Page numbers in **bold** indicate main references.

127

INDEX

INDEX